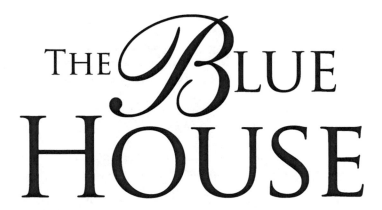

THE BLUE HOUSE

MICHAEL SIMMONS

with Dr. Daniel Middlebrooks

THE BLUE HOUSE

Scripture taken from the New King James Version®. Copyright © 1982 by Thomas Nelson. Used by permission. All rights reserved.

Scripture taken from The Holy Bible, King James Version. Cambridge Edition: 1769; King James Bible Online, 2017. www.kingjamesbibleonline.org.

iUniverse books may be ordered through booksellers or by contacting:

iUniverse
1663 Liberty Drive
Bloomington, IN 47403
www.iuniverse.com
1-800-Authors (1-800-288-4677)

ISBN: 978-1-5320-2160-2 (sc)
ISBN: 978-1-5320-2161-9 (hc)
ISBN: 978-1-5320-2162-6 (e)

Library of Congress Control Number: 2017907141

Print information available on the last page.

iUniverse rev. date: 05/09/2017

CONTENTS

ACKNOWLEDGMENTS

The first person to hear my life stories and the first person to encourage me to share them through this book was my wife, Jenny. She has been instrumental in proofreading and making valuable editing suggestions throughout this eighteen-month process. Often, as I became overwhelmed with the procedure of writing, she prayed with me and reminded me of the original intent of this project. Thank you, Jenny, for your gentle spirit and spiritual resolve for me.

I want to thank Dr. Robert Engelken for assistance with proofreading and offering suggestions for modifications of the earlier stages of the book. Dr. Engelken recently retired as a professor of electrical engineering after thirty-four years as a faculty member at Arkansas State University–Jonesboro and a career in engineering education and student-intensive research in photovoltaic materials and renewable energy. He and his family have also experienced numerous instances of God's divine providence and intervention in their lives.

Thanks to KD Fleming, award-winning author of the Pemberly series, *Campaigning for Love*, *Capturing the Minister's Heart*, and *Her Hometown Hero*, for her time and for sharing her writing and editing experience. She showed me how to turn the words on the page into the very beats of my heart within this story and the memories of my childhood. She opened my eyes to the true power of words and encouraged me to invite readers on this journey back to the Blue House and beyond. I will always be grateful for God's providence in causing our paths to cross.

Last, I want to thank Dr. Daniel Middlebrooks for his friendship before this book was birthed and for his time in writing the applications to open the reader's heart to the endless possibilities of God's grace. My thanks also to his sister-in-law, Tanya Middlebrooks, for her dedicated assistance in proofing and providing insights that helped the applications reach out and touch everyone.

INTRODUCTION

The purpose of this book is not to make myself look good or bad. As you will soon find out, the real hero is the Lord Himself. My number-one priority is to remind us that God has a purpose in His children's lives. Many people like to talk about luck or coincidence; I have come to realize in a Christian's life it is all about God's plan and life lessons. He opens and closes doors as He wills. He brings us into contact with people, places, and things that ultimately build our character and transform us into the people He desires us to be. At the end of each chapter, Dr. Middlebrooks has written "Life Lessons" to help stimulate an immediate response to what was experienced in the chapter. These lessons were included to broaden individual reflection or to serve as a guide for group bible study classes. Please keep in mind there are no right or wrong answers to the question in the study guide. These lessons are merely to encourage personal reflection, creative thinking, and open dialogue.

You have probably figured out by now this must be a lifelong process, and you would be exactly right. This process involves many ups and downs, twists and turns, and—oh yes—mistakes and wrong decisions on our parts. There will be many regrets, sleepless nights, and prayers asking God for help because we tend to mess up. We often find ourselves in situations we don't know how to handle. Sometimes this sidetracks our lives for months and often years because of our stubborn attitudes and refusal to confess our mistakes. If you are nodding your head and experiencing flashbacks of events and situations in your life that you wish you had handled differently, relax; you are not alone.

I want you to think of your life as a large puzzle where each piece represents significant events. You can look at your puzzle any time you wish, but your life puzzle is not complete until your life is over.

As I assemble my life's puzzle, I see pieces I would like to change, but there is one piece I am most proud to display. It was when, at a very young age, I asked Jesus to come into my life. After I became a believer and accepted the Bible as truth, the pieces of my lifelong puzzle began to change for the better. Through time and with God's help, I began to recognize corrections I needed to make. Each story in this book will create a new piece to be added to the puzzle of my life.

I am happy to say God is faithful. He always has been, and I know He always will be. I have learned through real-life events that I have a friend in Jesus, and He knows my name. His love for me is unstoppable, and the older I get the more I want to please Him. I have learned that I can't do anything to make Him love me more, and I can't do anything to make Him love me less. He loves me—period! The good news is, He loves you too, and His Word tells us He is not willing for any of us to perish.

The primary purpose of this book is to persuade you to place your trust in God and allow Him to guide you through the assembling of your lifelong puzzle. You can accomplish this by asking Him to be the Lord of your life. God loves us in spite of ourselves and shows His love as He directs our lives. Frequently, we don't recognize what God is doing. We may even become embittered or angry toward God, asking, "Why did You let this happen?"

I can assure you He is very much aware of every situation and is working continually to groom and prepare colorful pieces that will add beauty and completion to our life's puzzles.

I hope you enjoy this book and the life-changing stories that will introduce you to the God I love and the God who loves you beyond measure.

CHAPTER 1

The Box Top

EARLY PIECES

The year was 1957, and I was six years old. My family moved into what became known as the Blue House. When I was a kid, this was my most favorite house. It wasn't the nicest house on the block, but it had a fresh coat of blue paint, and to me it stood out as something special. This blue house was located directly across from the yellow elementary school building in Walnut Ridge, Arkansas. Lots of things happened in our neighborhood, and I made it my business to oversee them all.

There was a playground across the street from the Blue House, where the older boys would gather in the afternoons to play baseball. I was always hanging out on the sidelines with my ball glove in hand. I never actually got to play because the older boys felt I was too young. My job was to chase down the out-of-bounds balls, and that was good enough for me. I just wanted to be part of their group and felt thankful for the chance to hang out with the older guys.

This was a happy time in my life; I literally didn't have a worry in the world. That would soon change for me and my family, but for then, my time was consumed with school and playing in the yard every afternoon until Mother called me in for supper.

I remember eating supper quickly and then begging Mother to let me go back outside to play for those last few minutes before dark. Dusk/dark was a great time of the day to catch lightning bugs and to smell the magical scent of burning leaves. People in the neighborhood would rake their leaves into the ditches and burn them. It was a different world in 1957; burning leaves in town today would probably get you arrested. I still enjoy the scent of burning leaves; it makes me feel young and reminds me of a simpler time of life when everything seemed right in my world. I loved those days, living out the American dream in a small town in northeast Arkansas.

I believe God gives us windows of opportunity to catch hold of what we remember as the simple things in life. Often these simple things become our most cherished memories. We can revisit these happy times when we need a chuckle or a break from the grind of everyday struggles.

Usually these memories don't cost us anything, other than taking the time to enjoy them. We can deposit them into our memory banks and withdraw them when times get hard. I like to refer to them as "God's little gifts," and they always seem to bring a smile to my face.

THE "WHO" IN YOUR LIFE

I remember one afternoon when Mother was ironing clothes, and I was watching—or more likely aggravating—my two-year-old sister, Cindy. Often while Mom ironed clothes, she had time to answer questions that I had about all sorts of things. I was a very inquisitive child.

I remember asking Mother if we were rich. She laughed and said, "No! We are not rich, but we are not poor." I asked how much money Dad made, and, to my surprise, she told me he made seventy-five dollars per week. I had no concept of whether this was good or bad, but it satisfied my curiosity and I don't remember ever bringing it up again.

Dad was a television repair man, working for Burrow Hardware, a TV repair shop in Walnut Ridge. He would drive the company truck home with the advertisement on the side panel. Sometimes my older brother (by fifteen months), Tony, and I would go with Dad on service calls. If Dad couldn't fix the customers' TV sets in their homes, we would take the sets to his shop for further repair. I felt important, making those service calls with Dad because I thought we were really helping him with his job.

I liked being with Dad, and I think he enjoyed showing us boys his knowledge of electronics. Dad had strict rules for us to obey. The consequences for breaking his rules were severe and swift, with no talking or negotiating. The two-inch belt strapped around his waist did all his talking, if you get my drift.

There were two rules in our house, and we knew not to break them: (1) do not knock on the bathroom door when

3

occupied by Dad, and (2) do not disturb Dad when he is reading the Saturday newspaper.

One Saturday morning I began thinking how great it would be to have a lemon cookie from Dolly Smith's corner store. The store was located across the street from the school building and only three houses down from ours. At the time, though, it seemed that the store was located a long distance away. Mr. Smith enjoyed a good business in the corner store, and the big jar on his counter was always full of fresh-baked lemon cookies. I had two problems that I needed to overcome. The cookies were one penny each but I had no money, which led to my other problem—Dad was reading the paper.

I decided to bring my brother, Tony, into the picture. I thought it would be better if he, being older than me, asked Dad for the money. Unfortunately, Tony disagreed. This put me back to square one.

As I thought about how to approach Dad with my request, I decided to walk up to him, stand there, and wait for him to ask me what I needed. I moved forward with the plan, and it seemed like I stood in front of him for an hour. As I think back on the incident, however, I'm sure it was only a few minutes. Dad finally lowered his paper, and, with his dark brown eyes staring a hole through me, he asked what I wanted. I started my sales pitch by telling him that Mr. Smith had the best lemon cookies in town, they were always so fresh, and they were only one penny. I said, "I'll walk down and get us all one if you want me to."

Dad slowly raised the paper to cover his face and did not say a word. As I started to retreat, thinking my best sales pitch hadn't worked, much to my surprise he reached in his pocket and handed me a nickel. He said, "Get five cookies." Dad turned to Tony and said, "Go with your brother."

As we walked out the front door and down the concrete steps, we were on cloud nine. I said to Tony, "We have the best daddy in the whole world!"

PLANTING YOUR FEET AND HEART

Life is an amazing adventure for a six-year-old kid or a seventy-five-year-old man. Things change so quickly; you can be on cloud nine one day, and the next day you feel like the rug has been pulled out from under your feet.

A few weeks after the success of the cookie plan, I came home from school and found Mom on the couch, crying. This was not the norm at our house. Mom was always laughing and in good spirits. To see her crying, I thought surely someone had died.

When I asked Mom what was wrong, she quickly sent me to my room without any explanation. I stopped in the hallway, and from my vantage point I could see Mom on the couch and Dad sitting in his chair, the same chair where he'd been sitting when he gave me the nickel for the cookies. It was the same chair where he'd been sitting when I proclaimed him to be the best dad in the whole world.

I could hear them talking, and Mom said to Dad, "You call her; she's your sister." Dad responded, "She won't do it for me, but she will for you and the kids." I had no idea what was happening, but I was determined to figure it out, so I kept listening. Mother picked up the phone and dialed long distance to Seattle, Washington, for Mrs. Ruby Pickle, the name I recognized as my dad's sister.

After a short conversation, Mom explained to Ruby that my dad, Freddy Burl—her brother—was in trouble and needed help. Mom told her that Dad had been given a ticket for DWI. It's now called DUI— "driving under the influence"—but in 1957, DWI meant "driving while intoxicated." I couldn't make out everything Mom said, but through her sobs I heard her say that Dad had been driving his company's truck.

Dad had lost his job, and we did not have the money to pay the fine to keep him out of jail. She asked Aunt Ruby for $175. My aunt Ruby was always a generous person, and she agreed to send the money. Many years later, Mom told me that Dad had another woman in the company truck and wrecked the vehicle. I did not realize at the time, but this incident would be the first movement up the incline of a bad roller-coaster ride that would last many years for my family and me.

Do you remember when you fully realized that life was not always peaches and cream? For me, this realization came a few weeks later. I came home one afternoon and knew something was terribly wrong—I could just sense it. As I walked into the hallway, I looked into Mom and Dad's bedroom. I saw that the big mirror on their dresser had been shattered to pieces. When I asked Mom what had happened, she responded, "Go to your room."

I think I spent half of my life in my room because of all the questions that came rolling out of my mouth; I wanted to know everything about everything. Given a little bit of information, I could usually figure out what was going on.

As I walked to my bedroom, I saw where Dad's shoe had landed on the top of the dresser, and I figured out what had happened. This was a different world for me; I had never experienced anything like this before. Little did I know this was just the tip of the iceberg.

CHOICES

It is amazing that through all the life-changing events, our family never went to church/ My grandparents, Tommy and Connie Baird, Mother's parents, were church-goers, but it was not part of our lives. Mother had taught Tony and me to say children's prayers before bedtime, but that was the extent of our worship experience. I knew Mother had attended the White Oak Church when she was a young girl, and I remember asking, during one of our many question-and-answer days, if God was real. She told me, "Yes, He is real." It was at that moment, as a six-year-old boy, I put God and Santa Claus in the same category—two guys I needed to know.

We moved from Arkansas to a small town in Missouri called Hayti. Dad got a job at a local hardware store. He was good at repairing things and would work on lawn mowers, assemble bicycles, and perform other odd jobs, as well as drive a delivery vehicle.

This lasted only a few months before Dad was fired for drinking on the job. There we were again—Dad out of a job and no money to pay bills—so our family moved to a small house out in the country, about seven miles from Walnut Ridge, Arkansas.

The move was definitely a change of lifestyle. For the first time in my life, there was no bathroom in our house. There was running water in the kitchen for Mother to use for cooking but no toilet and no bathtub. How were we supposed to take our baths before bedtime? I soon learned that the pampered lifestyle we had always known—a nice house, lots of friends with whom to play, bathroom with a bathtub, and my asking if we were rich—was over. I certainly did not have to ask if we were rich any longer; I knew the answer. Reality had set in, and it was a different world for our entire family.

We moved into this house around October 1958. This month had always been my favorite time of year. I enjoyed the cool weather and the wonderful scent of burning leaves. The reality of our new life—of living in an old house with no bathroom facilities and a pot-bellied wood-burning stove for heat—suddenly set in. It especially became a reality when the cold winds of November brought the first nights of snow flurries. Anyone who has ever used an outdoor toilet in the winter can bear witness; it's not a pleasant experience. I don't even want to talk about the Sears and Roebuck catalog that soon replaced the roll of toilet paper.

Dad eventually got a job selling insurance, although he was not really successful at it. Money was tight. Mom and Dad didn't need to tell us kids that; we knew because there was limited food, and we stayed home from school several times because they didn't have the twenty cents needed for Tony or me to eat lunch in the school cafeteria.

Dad had started drinking heavily but not at home. Mother

would not allow that. One time he came into the house around one or two o'clock in the morning. I could hear them arguing in the living room. What used to be a home full of fun and laughter was now a house of arguing and many tears.

GIVERS AND TAKERS

By mid-November, with Christmas right around the corner, there was no money to buy even the bare necessities, much less Christmas presents. Tony, our baby sister, Cindy, and I asked Mother to take us to downtown Walnut Ridge to tell Santa Claus what we wanted for Christmas. It was only after I was grown that Mother told me the story of what she had done to make sure we had toys on Christmas morning.

In 1958, the main crops grown in Arkansas, where we were living, were cotton and soybeans. There was a cotton field right beside our house. Mother went to the field where the cotton pickers were working and explained to the man in charge that she needed to work to buy Christmas presents for her three young children. He told her she was welcome to pull cotton bolls, and the pay was two dollars per one hundred pounds. He offered to loan Mother a cotton sack.

The next morning after we had left for school, Mother went to the field to start her new job. Pulling bolls was different from picking cotton. Workers picked cotton in the autumn, but it was now mid-November, and the cotton had been picked more than twice. At this point, the whole boll was picked, and then the cotton gin would separate the cotton from the bolls.

It was cold in November, and by December of that year,

there was snow on the ground. I would come home from school and walk out to where Mother was working. She would be wearing a pair of brown cotton gloves to protect her hands from the sharp point of the bolls, but the fingers of the gloves were cut out so she could get a good grip around the bolls to pull them. The days were bitterly cold as the north wind would whistle through the cotton rows.

After working in the fields all day, Mother then cooked supper for the family. The skin on the tips of her fingers was cracked and bleeding as she tried to peel potatoes. After supper, Mom would wash the dishes, and one of us kids would dry, but when she put her hands in the hot soapy water, I could tell it was very painful.

At the time I didn't know why Mom was working in the fields. I had no idea she was saving her money to buy Christmas gifts for us kids. This was just one of the many times I saw my mother make sacrifices for her children.

When Mom came home from working in the fields, she would take her day's wages and carefully place them in a small red box in her dresser drawer. In those days, the farmers would pay their workers every day after the final weighing of the sacks of cotton. Many of the workers needed the money to buy food for their families that day. Living from hand-to-mouth was the norm for most of the workers.

An average woman could pull about three hundred pounds a day, which would pay six dollars, and some men could pull upwards of five hundred pounds, making ten dollars daily. I have no idea what Mom earned, but little by little she saved enough money to buy her children some Christmas presents.

I was excited when I arrived home from school at the start

of Christmas vacation—we had two weeks off from school. What a happy day! As I walked into the house and glanced into Mom and Dad's bedroom, I noticed their dresser drawers were pulled out and had been emptied on the floor. I called out for Mother, but the house was silent. I ran out into the backyard, where I could see the workers in the distant field, and then ran as hard and as fast as my legs would carry me until I reached Mom. Gasping for breath, I told her that the drawers in her bedroom were emptied all over the floor.

I will never forget the look on her face—a look of anguish mixed with the pain of a deep sorrow. Her face was sunburned from working outside, her nose was red on the tip from the cold, and her lips were chapped and cracked. I could see the tears welling up in her eyes. I always thought of Mother as being a pretty woman—no wrinkles and with a pretty smile. She was still pretty, but I could see that time spent working outside, coupled with the stress in her life, had added years to her appearance.

Mom didn't say a word to me but told the man in charge she needed to go home. When he asked if everything was okay, she nodded her head, but the obvious answer was no. He offered to weigh her sack of cotton bolls and promised to bring her wages by the house that afternoon. We headed home without talking, and I watched as Mom walked into the bedroom. She picked up her little red box, in which she had carefully stored her wages for the last several weeks. The box was empty! I saw the tears that she had managed to hold back start to fall as she put her hand to her mouth to control her sobs. At that point, I began to cry, not for the loss of the money or the ransacked bedroom, but because I loved Mother, and for the first time in my life I felt real pain—Mother's pain—and I didn't know what to do. So I cried. She pulled me up into her arms and comforted me, as only the love of a mother could do.

I couldn't completely understand the depth of her pain because I didn't know the full story. I didn't know she was saving money so her children could have presents under the tree on Christmas morning. I didn't understand that all her hard work in the fields to furnish a happy Christmas for her children now was all in vain, and she had no backup plan. I didn't know what she knew (which she shared with me many years later)—that Dad had staged a break-in but had taken the money himself and spent it at the local tavern.

Mother spent the next few days before Christmas trying to figure out how to tell her children that there would be no Christmas that year. She decided to wait until Dad got home on Christmas Eve so they could talk to us kids together.

I'm happy to say, for Mother's sake, that the talk never took place because on Christmas Eve, Dad sold a life insurance policy, and his company paid him his commission. He used the money to buy us boys our Fanner 50 cap gun and holster, caps, and a red cowboy hat. Cindy got her baby doll and a stroller. With sacks of apples and oranges under the tree, Christmas was a big success. In my seven-year-old mind, Santa Claus had come through, and all was well on Christmas morning. In reality, God and my sweet mother were the real heroes in our lives.

THE CRACK OF CHARACTER

Soon after Christmas, Dad came home with the bad news that he had been fired. Yes, he was unemployed again, but this time it wasn't for drinking on the job. No, this time he had some problems for which he might have to go to jail. We kids didn't understand everything that was going on at the time, but we knew something had caused Dad to really be concerned.

Many years later, Mother told us the real story. It seems that Dad had been forging people's names to insurance papers. He would sell someone a cheap life insurance policy. It looked like a good deal and was at a great price. When he got home, he would place the inexpensive policy under a clear glass and place a more expensive policy on top of the glass. Carefully, with pen in hand, he would forge the person's signature onto the more expensive policy. He would then turn in the expensive policy to his company and collect the higher commission.

I cannot say how Dad talked his way out of this jam, but the company decided not to press charges, and Dad was back looking for a new job.

There was a period when Mom and Dad would leave us with Grandmother and Grandpa Baird, Mom's parents. They were nice to us, but Grandpa Baird didn't care much for Dad. This was probably for good reason, but I didn't like him saying negative things about Dad in front of me. I heard Grandpa tell Mother that Dad was a drunk and would never amount to anything good. He offered to help her financially if she would leave him, but she said no, and at that time I didn't want her to leave.

At this point in my life, I felt very insecure. I remembered back, when we lived in the Blue House, I did not have a care in the world, no problems at all. Now, things were different. When my parents left us kids with our grandparents for a few days, I was so afraid that I would never see them again. I imagined they would be killed in a car wreck or just never come back for us. The mind of an eight-year-old boy can run wild, and mine certainly did. I worried about money—or rather, the lack of it. I worried about not having a house in which to live, I worried about Mother and Dad while they were gone, including where they would sleep and what they would eat. I worried about things that an eight-year-old should never have to be concerned. I felt myself withdrawing from people, not wanting to talk to them. After all, in my mind I asked, *Why would anyone want to talk with me?*

I don't believe my parents ever realized the psychological trauma I was experiencing. My life had been turned upside down, and I felt alone and without a way out of this shell that I felt closing up around me. I truly felt frightened, alone, and abandoned, without even one friend to whom I could turn—not one!

1

Life Lessons

When you purchase a puzzle, you generally buy it because of what you see on the box top. Once you open the box, each piece represents a unique place and perspective of life and growth. In each chapter of this book, Michael Simmons puts into place several life pieces that provide a small picture of his life. Each piece tells a multitude of stories—some happy, some sad, some good, and some bad but all a part of his life.

I would venture to guess that his pieces could also be yours and mine. Although stories and characters may be different, the life lessons are closely the same. It is a powerful picture that we will watch come together as each story fits into the unique shape of his life's puzzle. At the conclusion of each chapter, you will be provided a number of "Life Lessons" to coincide with the previous chapter. These lessons, as Mike stated earlier in the introduction, can be used for personal reflection or group conversation. There are no right or wrong answers because each reader provides their own personal backdrop for the box top of their life. All scripture quoted in these lessons are from the New King James Version of the Bible unless otherwise noted, now Let's take the pieces of Mike's life and see if his box-top picture resembles anything in our life pictures.

Early Pieces

In memories, less will always bring about more.

When you recall a cherished childhood memory, what is the object of the event? It is usually not located in the vastness of the picture but the simple fragment that captures your thoughts and creates a kaleidoscope of memories. Parents try to plan big events for and with their children but can quickly forget that it is about the "be with me" moments in a child's life. For Mike, moments like baseball, burning leaves, and the Blue House became an anchoring point in his life that helped bring calm in chaotic times. These are precious parental moments. These are also priceless God moments. He whispers in our ears, "I love you! Did you know that?" It is our response to that statement that can open us to the abundant life to thrive (see John 10:10) or cause us to recoil and wither away.

What are some of your favorite childhood memories? Which one is most special, and why? How did this memory impact your life? Are you willing to share the impact with others?

The "Who" in Your Life

It is not what you have but who has
you that makes you rich.

In the famous Dr. Seuss story *Horton Hears a Who*, we discover a character who not only needed a friend but who was willing to do whatever it took to protect the friend. Let me ask you the same question that Mike asked his mom: "Are you rich?" To answer that question, take this simple survey:

1. Do you equate wealth with possessions or people?
2. Do you have your best friend's or your financial accountant's cell number memorized?
3. Would you suffer a deeper loss in losing a best friend or a boat?
4. If you saw a need and had the resources to meet that need, would you give it and praise God for the opportunity, or would you pray for God to give someone else the opportunity?

Here are some of the "rich" moments Mike experienced in his childhood:

- a mother wealthy in patience
- a dad who was gracious with a gift of time and treats
- a young man who became brave by facing his fear

Read Matthew 6:21. Which character most resembles you? Why?

Planting Your Feet and Your Heart

In life, it is not where you stand but who stands with you that matters.

As a child, I watched cartoons with people riding a flying carpet. I always wondered what would happen if the carpet was pulled from under them. Ever felt that way? Mike described the "cloud nine" moments followed by a fall back into a painful reality. What is that carpet-stealing, song-snatching, panic-producing culprit? *Life!* Life can take your serene routine and turn it into a chaos.

What was one of your falls? What made it chaotic for you? How did it impact you and others around you? What did you do about it?

It is true that we often do not choose our circumstances. We do, however, choose how we are going to go through them and, most important, with whom. Consider Hebrews 13:5b when you enter a time of struggles: "For He Himself [Jesus] has said, 'I will never leave you nor forsake you.'"

What does this promise mean to you? What does it teach you about commitment and confidence? What other promises like this can you find in scripture?

Choices

The choices in our lives rarely ever impact only us.
They almost always impact others.

Do you like multiple-choice tests? Pass or fail, it was your grade to bear. Wouldn't it be great if all the choices you made in life impacted only you and no one else? The problem is, that usually is not the case. Take a moment to consider a simple illustration found in Galatians 6:7–8. As you read these words, answer these questions:

- What "bad crop" did you experience in your life due to the wrong choices of others?

- What sad seeds have you sown that might have reaped a hurtful harvest in another's life?
- What are you willing to do to seek restitution and reconciliation for these seeds (or shoes) you have thrown?

Givers and Takers

In life there will be givers and takers. The one we choose will either lead to a legacy of life or a liability in life.

We are challenged to seek what it truly means to be a giver in life. One speaker said, "You make a living by what you get. You make a life by what you give." Mike's mom became a vivid picture for him of this statement, and she also embodied for him the Proverbs 31 woman. How did Mike's mom reflect the principles of a giver, as found in Proverbs 30:10-12, 15-17, and 25-28 (KJV)? Allow me to leave you with the ultimate picture of a giver, Jesus Christ, who said, "The son of man did not come to be served but to serve and give His life as a ransom for many" (Matthew 20:28, JKV). There will be those who are giving heroes in your life. The question is, will you be one of them?

The Crack of Compromise

Compromise is the small crack in one's character that can lead to a fissure-type future.

How much is your character worth? Have you ever heard the phrase, "Everyone has his price"? In Genesis 3:1–6 (NKJV), we discover a threefold technique that serves to chip away at a person's character and reputation—manipulation, rationalization, and justification. In the story of Mike's dad and the life insurance policies, what would you have done? If we do wrong things for the right reasons, are they still wrong in God's eyes? In the end, compromise will not only lead to a crack in the character, but it will become a fissure-size failure in the future.

A life of integrity creates not only a strong position for life, but it also leaves a legacy of power for others in our lives. Children watch what their parents do, hear what they say, and reflect who they are. Will your children grow confident and secure in who they are or insecure in what will happen next? Consider these scriptures—Jeremiah 29:11, Matthew 11:28–29, Philippians 4:19 (NKJV)—and ask yourself if you trust your heavenly Father in these promises.

CHAPTER 2

Pieces of Hurt and Hope

FAITHFUL FARMERS

Mom and Dad were gone a lot. Tony and I stayed with our grandparents, Tommy and Connie Baird, while our sister, Cindy, went with our parents on the road. When Mom would tell us she and dad were leaving, I would beg her to stay. One day she explained to me the reason they left was to look for a job for Dad, and soon everything would be okay. She promised we would soon have our own place to live, and things would be like they were when we lived in the Blue House. That was exactly what I needed to hear; I believed everything Mother said, and from then on, I put all my hopes and dreams in that one basket.

Staying with Grandmother and Grandpa Baird wasn't bad. They were loving people, especially Grandmother. She was sweet and kind, always laughing, and would often wrestle with us boys. I loved that about her, especially when she would hold us down and sit on us. Her height was all of five foot one, but she did her part and then some around the farm.

Grandmother was a great cook. She didn't make snacks or sandwiches for meals; she cooked three big meals every day. This was a working farm, and Grandpa believed in eating three square meals. Grandmother was up at dawn and didn't stop working until the last dish was washed and put away. I never heard her complain about anything.

Grandpa was a stern man; the word *love* was not commonly in his vocabulary. He had a good heart but didn't show much affection to us kids, although he did show it to Grandmother. Grandpa was a diabetic and took a shot of insulin after breakfast every morning. Grandmother administered the shot, and afterward, Grandpa would kiss her and tell us kids that the kiss was his dessert. I always liked Grandpa's doing that, and I could tell it made Grandmother feel special.

Tony and I would do little jobs around the farm, and Grandpa, being a fair man, always paid us for the work we did. He was also an honest man and loved to talk about his days as a military policeman in the army during World War II. What I enjoyed most was when he would get out his box guitar. He loved to strum, and on occasion, we could persuade him to sing. He knew some funny songs. We would all gather around while he entertained us. One of my favorite songs went like this:

> Now boys gather round, take a tip from me
> I'm sure that you will all agree
> If you let a girl fool you with fate
> You'll soon be swinging on a golden gate

You'll miss out on all the fun if you love only one
So you better take heed to my little song
Find 'em, fool 'em, and leave 'em alone

GRACE AND GRIT

One thing I always admired about my grandparents was that they were church-goers. I heard stories about Grandpa when he was a younger man. He ran a hamburger joint, where he also sold beer. I was told that it was a pretty rough place, but I didn't know anything about those days.

At this point in their lives, however, they always went to church on Sunday morning, and if Tony and I were at their house, we went to church also. This church thing was all kinds of strange to me. I didn't quite understand everything the preacher said. Grandpa talked a lot about God blessing them with good crops, and he spoke about God always making a way for them to have a good life. I stayed quiet, but like most young children, my ears were open, taking in everything that Grandpa said about God. I had a million questions I would have liked to ask, but I didn't. I usually got sent to my room when I started asking too many questions.

I was curious about this God of whom they talked, and I wondered if He would help my family. All I knew were the children's prayers that Mother taught us to say at night. I didn't understand. I thought someone needed to explain to God that Dad needed a job, and we needed a house. I had a whole list of things I needed God to work on. I was thinking like a lot of folks I know today, always asking God for things they need or want but never thanking Him for what they already have.

I was confused and couldn't quite figure out what to do. I didn't feel comfortable going to my grandparents with my questions. What I needed was one of those days back in the Blue House, when Mother would answer my questions while she ironed clothes. I could ask all the questions necessary to get this praying thing straight in my mind. I thought about my options and decided to hold everything until I could get with Mother.

FLEETING FAITH

That weekend Mom and Dad pulled up in front of my grandparents' house with the big news: Dad had a new job. They had already rented a house, and we were moving to a town in Arkansas called Jonesboro.

Jonesboro is a college town, home to Arkansas State University, and it was the largest town in which our family had ever lived. The new house was located on Case Street. It had indoor plumbing, three bedrooms, a bathroom, a living room, and an eat-in kitchen. We were living high, and I wondered if God had anything to do with helping out our family. I had not forgotten how Grandpa would talk about God supplying all of their needs. This was a fleeting thought, however; because in my eight-year-old mind, I questioned how God could have had a part in something about which He and I hadn't talked. How could He know what we needed?

I thought about asking Tony. He usually could answer any questions I had. In this case, however, I thought it might be better to discuss this issue with Mom.

Tony was a reader; he loved reading comic books and

had an entire collection. He loved reading science fiction but would read nearly anything he could get his hands on. I tried reading some of his comic books, but that wasn't for me. I needed to be outside playing ball or fishing in that little ditch out back. Tony was the brains, and I was the brawn; that's been the case for most of our lives.

We settled in to our new house.; Dad had a job at Barnhill's Hardware and everything was working out great. I met a lot of neighborhood boys, and we had a lot of fun exploring the general area. The only thing holding me back was that I had no wheels. I needed a bike! Most of the guys had bikes, so that's what I asked Mom and Dad to get me for Christmas that year.

A TALE OF FOUR EYES

School started in August. I was beginning the third grade. I was still suffering from a poor self-image; it was hard for me to make friends at a new school because most of the kids knew each other from the previous year, and I was a bit of an outsider.

I also had a problem at school because of poor eyesight. I struggled with not being able to see what was written on the blackboard. The glasses my parents bought for me were relatively worthless. No one would believe me when I said I couldn't see any better with the glasses than I could without them. I found out many years later that I had a lazy eye, and I was only clearly seeing from one eye. My childhood doctor, who was not a specialist, put a prescription lens in both sides of the glasses, which totally confused my brain. I needed a good ophthalmologist, but in those days, that didn't happen.

This eye problem didn't do much for my self-image. My teacher, Mrs. Swinney, was determined that I needed to wear my glasses all the time. I would take them off, and some of the kids would tattle: "Mrs. Swinney, Mike has his glasses off." She would scold me in front of the other kids, and I would put them on again. I am sure she meant well, but it was humiliating to me, so I made up a song, "Way down upon the Suwanee River sits Mrs. Swinney on her fanny."

I thought it was a great song, but I knew that Mom, Dad, or any of the kids at school had better never hear me sing that one. Still, it was my own private song, and singing it in front of the mirror at home gave me great pleasure. Sometimes I would add a few choice words that I wanted to say to her.

I think we all had times as kids when we were bold—in the bathroom, with the door closed and locked. It was a private place where we could respond to people that rubbed us the wrong way. If you still practice this technique, I say go for it!

BRIGHT DAYS AND DARK NIGHTS

Thanksgiving rolled around, and school let out for an entire week. All I could think about was that it was only six weeks until Christmas. All I wanted to talk about was that new bike I wanted—actually needed, if I was to stay in good standing with the other boys in the neighborhood.

Dad was doing pretty well with his new job at the hardware store. His drinking had cooled down, and everything seemed good from my perspective. He was working every day, and our family life seemed to have returned to normal.

The only problem I was having was with my self-image. I felt like I was living on the edge of a cliff, and I could fall off at any moment—although I honestly couldn't tell you to where I would fall or from what. At times, I just felt afraid—a sense of insecurity. Don't get me wrong; I was playing with the other guys in the neighborhood, but at night, after I went to bed, I felt afraid and lonely. There was a void in my life that I did not understand. I felt insecure, for sure, but I never told anyone. I put on a good front because I didn't want anyone to know about the real me.

Sadly, I think many people, as adults, experience some of the same feelings I had as a child—loneliness, even when they are surrounded by so-called friends; insecurities with their jobs; the pressures of life; and no security for what tomorrow will bring. It doesn't matter whether we are young or grown up; these thoughts can wreak havoc on our minds. If we don't have someone or something other than ourselves in whom to trust, life can be a lonely place.

FREEDOM

Christmas finally came, and, man, that new bike was amazing. I had the prettiest bike in the neighborhood. We got up before dawn and had Christmas gift-giving. Mother fixed breakfast, but I couldn't eat. All I could think of was getting on the street with my new bike.

Daylight came, but with it was a completely overcast sky, with a slight drizzle of sleet. I begged Mom and Dad to let me just take one trip up the street and back, just to get the feel of the new red bike under my body. It would be a dream come true. They agreed, so I mounted the bike and rode out of the yard and onto the street. I immediately hit a patch of ice. *Bam!* Down I went—hard—on the pavement. I was up in a flash, checking out the bike. Everything was well, and I took off down the street, feeling freedom at last with my own wheels. I was overjoyed as I breathed the cold air and felt the sleet as it stung my uncovered face. My hand was bleeding where I'd shielded myself in my fall, but I couldn't have cared less about my wounds or the weather condition. I had a new bike, and all was well in my little world.

To say I enjoyed my new bike would be an understatement. I couldn't wait to get home from school in the afternoon because the bike was waiting for me to embark on a new adventure. I loved the freedom it brought to my life. I can still envision the wind pinning my hair back as I flew down the street. It was exhilarating!

GOD APPOINTMENT

Once winter was gone, we enjoyed the spring and wearing short-sleeved shirts and no jackets. It was perfect weather for cruising. On one particular day, I was enjoying my daily ride up and down the road when I noticed an elderly woman walking from her porch out to the edge of the street. (I laugh as I write about her being "elderly" because she wasn't much older than I am today.) She was probably around seventy, but to an almost-nine-year-old, she looked old. I saw her sitting on her porch on several occasions, but I never gave it much thought. She lived in a small duplex in the middle of the block. I had no idea that this lady—I'd soon know her as Mrs. Tompkins—would change my life in a very real way.

As I look back today and apply what I know now, I realize that this is exactly the way God works in our lives. God does some of His best work when we least expect it! He brings people, places, and things together at just the right moment to achieve His overall design for our lives.

I can't explain God—trying to explain God would be like trying to pour the ocean into a small bucket—but I do understand that God knows what He is doing, and we need only to have faith in Him and move on with our lives. That's why it is so important for us, as Christians, to obey the Spirit when He prompts us to do something. It is a biblical truth that, if you are a Christian, God has a special plan for your life. He has things for you to do that only you can accomplish and people only you can reach. You will see later in this book how this rang true in my life, but for now, let's get back to Mrs. Tompkins and see what God was preparing to do through that beautiful lady.

A VOICE IN OUR WILDERNESS

As I slowed my bike, this elderly lady started waving her hand, flagging me down. I'd never spoken to her or even met her, but I pulled over to see what she wanted. All kinds of bad things ran through my mind; surely I must have done something wrong. In a moment, however, this sweet little lady completely put my mind at ease and won me over by saying these few words: "That surely is a beautiful bike."

Well, obviously, this was a very smart lady. She knew a bike of quality when she saw one. I immediately told her that I had received "her" (the bike) for Christmas and that I polished her every day after school. I explained that I never left her out in the rain but kept her on our front porch. She listened with interest to what I had to say, and I must admit I liked this lady. She won me over by simply letting me talk about something that was of interest to me. Pretty good tactic, wouldn't you say?

In a little bit, she told me her name was Mrs. Tompkins. I liked that name, and I liked her. It was as if we had been friends for a long time. She asked me some questions about the other boys in the neighborhood. She wanted to know if I knew them, so I told her I did, and then I told her who lived in each house up and down the block. She asked other questions that I found very easy to answer.

"Do you like Kool-Aid?"

"Yes," I replied.

"How about popcorn and candy?"

"Of course," I added.

She then told me that she was planning a little get-together—she called it Sunbeam—every Thursday afternoon at four o'clock, and all the children in the neighborhood were invited. "Do you go to church?" she asked.

"I don't," I told her, "but my grandmother and grandpa do."

"Do you know any of the stories from the Bible?"

"I know some," I answered. "Mom taught me."

"I'm going to be reading from a Bible storybook during Sunbeam," she said, "and afterward, we'll have refreshments. Is that something you might enjoy?"

"Yes!"

"Will you help me get the word to the other children in the neighborhood?"

"Of course, I replied."

I didn't know it then, but that was my first missionary experience. God was at work in my life, although I didn't know to what extent.

SHINING SUNBEAM

I spread the word to the neighborhood boys, and when I got home that day, I told Mother what had happened. She walked down to talk to Mrs. Tompkins, and after their visit, Mom told me it would be okay for me to go on Thursdays to Sunbeam. I was glad because I really wanted to go, and I was excited to have this new friend in the neighborhood. I didn't know that I would soon learn to love and admire this wonderful Christian lady, someone who would soon introduce me to the God I desperately needed in my life, in order to face the many challenges that were destined to come my way.

As I look back over my life from today, as I write this in 2016, to the year 1959, I am amazed. I was a young boy, living from day to day, innocent of what would unfold in my life. As a young man, I had no clue how desperately I would need a relationship with the God of this universe, especially a God who would reach out to me within the next few weeks through my new friend, Mrs. Tompkins.

Just as amazing to me was Mrs. Tompkins, a woman with a servant's heart. She sat on her porch and watched us boys riding our bikes up and down the street, and she wondered what she, a seventy-four-year-old widow, could do for the Lord. It is a beautiful thing when you understand how God works. On one hand, there was a young boy who needed to hear about God, and on the other hand, there was a woman who was willing to share the Lord with others. God simply planted the thought in her heart to share with others about our great God, and suddenly Sunbeam was conceived.

A BUCKET FULL

Think about it like this: our great and magnificent God, in a very simplistic way, met the needs in Mrs. Tompkins's life as well as in mine. One of us was serving God while the other was learning to serve God. Don't you just love how God works all things together for good for those who love the Lord and are called according to His purpose?

God is not a complicated God, yet He is an unfathomable God at the same time. I seem to be trying to put the ocean in a child's bucket, but it simply can't be done. Here is where we must use words like *faith*, *trust*, and *love*. God made salvation so simple that the most uneducated person can receive His gift, while the most educated person can also receive it but can't totally explain it. If you feel that you need to understand God better to accept His gift of salvation, listen to what He said about Himself: "For my thoughts are not your thoughts, neither are your ways my ways, saith the LORD. For as the heavens are higher than the earth, so are my ways higher than your ways, and my thoughts than your thoughts" (Isaiah 55:8–9 KJV)

I don't understand everything about the sixty-five-inch

Samsung Curve Smart television that my wife bought me for my birthday, but I did not reject it and definitely will not send it back simply because I don't completely understand how it works. I have enjoyed every ball game we have watched on that TV set.

I worked hard over the next few days, telling the guys about what Mrs. Tompkins was planning with her gathering called Sunbeam. Some of the guys were unreceptive about the Bible stories, so I reverted to the tactics that were used on me—offering candy, popcorn, and Kool-Aid—and it worked. When Thursday rolled around, about eight of us guys were on her porch. When she invited us inside, I looked around. Everything was in place, and we were very quiet as we took our seats. It was a very small living room. Mrs. Tompkins took her place in front of us and said, "I am going to read from this Bible storybook, answer questions, and then offer some refreshments."

I don't remember which story Mrs. Tompkins read first, but I know I enjoyed it—I enjoyed them all. As time went on, the eight boys fell to six, and then to four. I tried to hold back on my questions; if I asked too many, the guys would become impatient waiting for the snacks. I asked her one day, when the attendance was low, if she was going to quit reading the stories if only a few boys came. "As long as one boy is present," she told me, "I will read." I hugged her around her waist and told her I would be there.

SWEET INVITATION

I was learning so much from the stories and from Mrs. Tompkins's answers. Some of the older ladies in the neighborhood had asked me to go to the corner store for them. They would give me a list of what they wanted and the money to pay for the groceries. One lady always wanted to pay me a nickel for the services. One day I told her I didn't want to be paid, that Mrs. Tompkins told us we should be kind to our neighbors.

She said, "If you don't take the nickel, then I can't let you go for me anymore." So I took the nickel. I always bought the same thing—a doughnut called a Long John Silver. It was a glazed jelly-filled donut, and, man, was it good. Other ladies in the neighborhood never offered to pay, so I appreciated the nickel and thought I would like to be more like the lady who paid when I grew up.

Some days I would see Mrs. Tompkins out on her porch, so I would stop by to sit on the steps and visit. I had a lot of questions, and she knew the answers. One day she asked if I wanted to go to the Church of the Nazarene with her. She told me the church bus would pick me up and bring me home. I told her I needed to ask Mom. After Mother agreed that I could go. I couldn't wait to tell Mrs. Tompkins the good news.

That Sunday, the church bus pulled up in front of the house and picked up Tony and me. Mrs. Tompkins was already on the bus. I enjoyed the ride through the neighborhoods. Since I wasn't allowed to go more than two blocks from my house on my bike, this was a real treat. When we got to church, a man took Tony and me to our Sunday school class. Our teacher's name was Bill Howard. I was very quiet in class and stuck by Tony's side. I knew he would understand everything that was going on. It was great having a big brother like Tony.

FISHER OF FUTURE MEN

Over time, I grew to love Bill Howard. He was a kind man, and I thought he was probably sort of like God Himself would be if I ever met Him. Bill Howard sometimes planned Saturday fishing trips for us boys, something I really loved. I became comfortable at church and Sunday school, and one Sunday morning, they had what was referred to as an altar call. I wanted to go forward. I had learned that I could be saved by asking Jesus to live in my heart, I wanted that—I needed that.

I wanted to go up front, but I was afraid. The church was so big, and the altar was so far away. For a nine-year-old boy who felt insecure, it took a lot to begin that journey. The first step was the hardest step I have ever taken, but it was the wisest move I ever made. I walked down the aisle, and, after a few steps, I felt a big, strong hand on my shoulder. I turned to look and saw it was my teacher, Bill Howard. I started to cry, and he walked with me and knelt beside me. He explained what accepting Jesus in my life meant, and after I said that I wanted to accept Him, we prayed. My life was forever changed that day. When I got home from church, I told Mom I had accepted Jesus as my Savior. She hugged me, and I saw tears in her eyes. Mom told me how proud she was of me, and I knew I had made the right decision—no doubt in my mind.

I had been saying a child's prayer that went like this:

> Now I lay me down to sleep,
> I pray the Lord my soul to keep.
> If I should die before I wake,
> I pray the Lord my soul to take.

Mother taught me the Lord's Prayer, and I felt proud to pray a grown-up prayer. I would lie in bed at night, segmenting and analyzing the words of my new prayer. I wanted to fully understand the words I was praying.

I still do that today and am amazed at what God reveals through prayers.

SHORT TIME BUT LONG LEGACY

I was devastated a few months later when Dad told us at the supper table that we were moving to a town called Weiner, Arkansas. He had decided to go into business for himself. Fred's TV Repair Shop would be the name of his business, and the building had already been rented. I remember going to Mrs. Tompkins's house to say good-bye, since I knew I would probably never see her again. I had grown to love her, and saying good-bye was difficult. I didn't have that many friends, and no one, not even Tony, was as smart as she was.

I have thought about those days and what this elderly woman taught me that enriched and changed my life forever. I have thought about the rewards waiting for her in heaven. I never saw her after that day, but I look forward to the time when we meet again. I have pondered the conversations we had while sitting on her front porch steps. I wonder if we will resume our conversations on her front porch steps in heaven. I know she will be proud that I remembered and followed up on what she taught me about God.

Who would have ever thought that fifty-seven years later, the eight-year-old she flagged down on Case Street in Jonesboro, Arkansas, would reach back in time and give her credit for introducing a group of young boys to the God she loved?

I'll tell you the truth: this amazing God we serve keeps up with everything about our lives. He has promised rewards for the times we simply give a thirsty person a cool glass of water to drink, not to mention the times we lead others in the Spirit to the Living Water. Doesn't that make you want to serve Him even more in this short span of time we call our earthly lives? To God be the glory!

2

Life Lessons: Pieces of Hope and Hurt

It is not what is in your hand at the end of
the day that counts. It is what is in your heart
at the end of your life that matters.

When you are putting a puzzle together, it's important to have the corner pieces in place. In this chapter, there were four people who represented the corner pieces in Mike's life. One corner piece stands for his grandparents, Tommy and Connie Baird. A second piece represents a tough teacher named Mrs. Swinney. A third piece is illustrated by a godly senior citizen, Mrs. Tompkins. The last corner piece is for a church teacher named Bill Howard. In the mixture of both hurt and hope, each corner piece was crucial in Mike's life. Let's examine each relationship to see how these people influenced Mike's life. As you do, ask yourself, "Who influenced my life?"

The Corner Piece of Gracious Grandparents: Faithful Farmers

The true goal of farming is not the planting of
crops but the production of faithful people.

When Mike and his brother, Tony, lived with their grandparents, the boys got an education not taught at any school. Mike learned to work hard and that a strong work ethic creates a strong character. What does it mean to you to work hard?

Mike also learned to laugh. Laughter pushes back the darkness of despair and brings in the light of life. When was the last time you laughed until you cried?

Next, Mike learned, through examples, to love deeply. The simple actions used to express love can say more than words. Tender actions are like the dessert in life, and the loving words are the cherries on top. It's been said that you can give without loving, but you cannot love without giving. What act of love have you given lately?

Finally, Mike learned to sing often. Songs can bring down barriers between people and connect generations. Singing is not as much a tune you sing as it is a melody in your heart. What is your favorite song? Why does it connect with you? Is your song a solo or a chorus of voices? Read Colossians 3:23. How does this scripture fit into these lessons?

Grace and Grit

The true measure of strength is not found in the power
of your muscles but in the passion of your motives.

When Mike went to live with his grandparents, he saw the beautiful picture of two people who came together in grit and grace. They were hard workers on the farm and faithful church-goers. Both had a strong resolve to provide, yet they had the time and tenderness to take care of two insecure boys. The grandparents took the boys to church and immersed them in a home-style faith. The best lessons are sometimes those spoken around the dinner table.

Has there been a time when you prayed a laundry list of needs in your life? What does the following verse mean to you? "For the LORD God is a sun and shield; the LORD bestows favor and honor. No good thing does he withhold from those who walk uprightly" (Psalm 84:11).

How can you become grit and grace in someone's life?

Fleeting Faith

To keep a problem before God in prayer
is to keep praise ready on our lips.

Mike experienced a special time with his grandparents as they poured God's truths into his heart and life. Mike struggled with thoughts of having to explain to God what he and his family needed. Have you ever felt that way? Do you ever explain to your heavenly Father the needs, the wants, and the desires in your life? Do you tell God your foolproof plan to solve the issue?

Read Matthew 6:8. In God's provision, Mike's family was blessed with a house that was able to replace the Blue House. Like us, Mike didn't know to say, "Thank you, God!" When was the last time you went before the Lord asked Him to meet a need? When was the last time you thanked God for providing for you? If you jot down all of the positives in your life, it will be a great focus for your next prayer.

The Corner Piece of a Tough Teacher: A Tale of Four Eyes

Children are wet cement. Be careful of the
imprints that you make in their hearts.

In Mike's childhood, classmates and an insensitive teacher caused humiliation. Mike used a made-up song that belittled his teacher to feel gratified, but it didn't last. Is this story your story? You may have a physical problem, like Mike's lazy eye, a speech impediment, or any self-image issue. Have you ever asked God, "Why did you make me this way?" Did you know that God calls you His *masterpiece* in Ephesians 2:10? The psalmist states in Psalm 139:14 that we are "fearfully and wonderfully made. Your works are wonderful." The cure for a lazy eye may be a good set of glasses, but the cure for a hurting heart, for sure, is God's amazing grace.

Bright Days and Dark Nights

The stillness of a lake does not denote
a bottom free of rocks.

When you throw a rock into a lake, what happens? Ripples travel out for a distance, and then everything goes back to normal. Is it really back to normal? The surface may have returned to its original state, but the lake has been changed. Why? The rock is at the bottom of the lake. For Mike, everything seemed to be going well for his family and friends, but Mike struggled with loneliness, fear, and emptiness. The apostle John describes a special light in 1 John 1:5–7. What is it? What does this mean to you? Mike had a fear of the unknown. What do you fear? What are you willing to do to overcome this fear? King David wrote, "Weeping may endure for a night, but joy comes in the morning" (Psalm 30:5).

The Corner Piece of a Saintly Servant: Freedom

Freedom in life is not doing what we want to do
but the ability to do what we should do.

Was there a special gift that you wanted one Christmas more than anything? In Mike's story, the new bike gave him a feeling of freedom. Even with the initial bumps and bruises, it was a glorious feeling for him as it would be for us all. Were there times when you felt the surge of freedom or the feeling that you could take on the world? Maybe it was when you got your first car, your first date, or your first job. How does that memory of freedom help you in tough times?

In the following lessons, you will take a ride with Mike as he travels the roads of his neighborhood to find an elderly lady who shows him what true freedom actually is. It was not the kind that came through spinning wheels; it came through spending time in God's Word.

God Appointment

When one is thirsty, a small cup of water can
go further than a big picture of an ocean.

Do you believe there are no chance meetings on "God appointments"? If you took that perspective every day, what impact would you make in the lives of others? What impact would they make in your life? Mike reminds us that the only way we will be able to experience these moments is through obedience. True godly obedience is following God's will before you realize His plans for you. In Genesis 12:1–3, Abram provides a strong example of godly obedience. Are you willing to do what God tells you to do, even when you don't know why? When was the last time you had to go on faith only?

A Voice in Our Wilderness

Warm words of love will always draw a cold soul.

Mike encountered a woman who had a welcoming home and a loving heart for children. Mrs. Tompkins used all she had to introduce the neighborhood kids to Jesus. Have you ever felt that God placed someone in your life to teach you about faith? Has God used you in someone's life to do the same? Colossians 3:12 states, "Therefore, as God's chosen people, holy and dearly loved, clothe yourselves with compassion, kindness, humility, gentleness and patience." How can you help someone today who needs Jesus?

Shining Sunbeam

The power of a light is found in two elements: first, in the source of the light; second, in the ability to be reflected.

When you light a candle in a dark room, your eyes go first to the flame. If you place the candle in front of a mirror, the light is reflected. The flame lights more places and goes other directions. After the invitation from Mrs. Tompkins, Mike became her mirror and reflected the love of Christ, as learned from Mrs. Tompkins, to those around him. Jesus called Himself the "Light of the world" (John 8:12). He calls you to "Let your light shine" (Matthew 5:16). Do you know that Jesus is the only true light in our dark world? If not, go to John 3:16 and Romans 3:23; 6:23; and 10:9–10,(NKJV) and talk with someone. If your answer is yes, how can you reflect Jesus's love today?

A Bucket Full

It is not what you put into a bucket that counts
but what you are willing to pour out.

Take a moment and read Jeremiah 29:11. Mike realized that we cannot limit God any more than we can put the ocean in a bucket. Have you ever tried to explain God or understand all that He does? Jeremiah tells us God's plan is to love us and bless us. Mike also reminded us that we serve a *big* God. What has God done for you that fills your life's bucket?

A Sweet Invitation

In a world filled with words that impact me, the sweetest
are those words that invite me to come and see.

As a child, did you ever get an invitation to a birthday party? As an adult, maybe you received one for a wedding or another special event. What did you do? It probably depended on the relationship you had with the person who invited you. Mrs. Tompkins invited Mike to go with her to church. She did this only after she had established a friendly relationship with Mike. She took the time to show Christ in her life so the invitation would be sincere and accepted. Is there someone with whom you have started a friendship that can make a way for you to invite that person to church? Do you live a godly life that provides the evidence of your sincerity?

The Corner Piece of a Fisherman: Fisher of Future Men

There are those who come into our lives and go quickly.
Then there are those who come and stay a while
and leave footprints on our hearts. Because
of them, we will never be the same.

Mr. Bill Howard helped Mike and his friends by teaching life lessons and sharing his faith. Fishing trips helped to open Mike's heart to God's presence. The Sunday school classes helped Mike to open his eyes to God's love. In the poem "Footprints in the Sand," there is a time when the narrator sees only one set of footprints. Have you experienced a time like that when God carried you? Did God use someone like Bill Howard to carry you? Paul reminds us in Romans 10:14–15 how important it is to be willing to share our lives and God's love. Bill's hand on Mike's shoulder helped support

Mike as Mike made his life decision to follow Christ. Has God used you in this way for someone else?

Short Time but Long Legacy

It is not the last step in our lives that
determines our destination but the first.

Have you ever placed your hands in wet cement? Why did you do it? Mike wrote these words: *Who would have ever thought that fifty-seven years later, the eight-year-old she flagged down on Case Street in Jonesboro, Arkansas, would reach back in time and give her credit for introducing a group of young boys to the God she loved?*

Both Mrs. Tompkins and Bill Howard took the time to impact the lives of neighborhood boys for Christ. Read 1 John 2:13. What imprints have you left in someone's life for the Lord? If you do not have someone, are you willing to start today? If so, with whom?

CHAPTER 3

Pieces of Right and Wrong

SHELL HOUSE

We made the move to Weiner in northeast Arkansas. Farming was the way of life there, and rice was the predominant crop. When leaving the downtown area of Weiner, all we could see for miles was rice crops and rice bins set up to store the harvest. Dad had rented a small building in the downtown area, and above the door was a sign painted in bold letters: FRED SIMMONS TV REPAIR SHOP. I could tell Dad was proud of his new business, and, by all accounts, it was doing very well. We found out Mom was pregnant; this would be the fourth addition to the Simmons family. The announcement was made but not discussed in detail. I did hear Mom and Dad talking about not having any medical insurance, and the cost of delivery was going to be around $150. The plan was for Mother to have the baby in the Jonesboro hospital; then Mother and we kids would spend a couple of weeks at our grandparents' house in Walnut Ridge.

Dad had moved our family into what was known back then as a "shell home." Jim Walter Builders would build the shell of a house on the owner's property, and the owner then was responsible for finishing the inside at his discretion. The owner contracted only for the shell, but the builders sold many homes like that because the price was right. We did not buy the house; we rented it. The house was located about eight miles from town, down a gravel road. It was built off the main gravel road, about a quarter mile down a dirt path.

Everything looked good until the first big rain; at that point, the whole area flooded. Our little dirt path leading to the main road was completely under water. Dad had to get a jon boat to transport us from our house out to the bus stop. We were living in a marsh, or swampy area, and it was a different experience for us. Mosquitoes were so thick in the air that we could hardly stand to be outside in the evening. The rice fields bred mosquitoes, and with the rains flooding the area, it was almost an unbearable place to live.

DIFFERENT DAY, SAME DAD

Dad had started drinking heavily, and most days when he came home from work, we could smell alcohol on his breath and clothes. Often, his speech would be a little slurred. I knew Mom would be aggravated with him, and we could hear them arguing in the kitchen. Dad, now self-employed, would drink in his shop during the day, and there was no one to tell him he couldn't.

Dad had a terrible temper when he was drinking, and he had a foul mouth to go along with it. Taking the Lord's name in vain was a normal part of his vocabulary, drinking or not. None of us kids liked being around Dad when he was drinking because we never knew what he was going to do.

I hated for Dad to take the Lord's name in vain. I knew it was wrong for him to talk that way, and I was determined it would never be part of my vocabulary. I missed going to church, and I missed listening to the preacher talk about God and how much He loves us. From the first moment I heard that message, it was as if it went straight from my ears through my brain and settled in my heart. Yes, I was just a boy, but I knew what Dad was doing was wrong and what the preacher had preached was right. I was determined to do what was right.

One day Dad came home from work, and I could tell that—as usual—he had been drinking. He decided he needed some cigarettes from the corner store about three miles away. Tony and I were playing in the yard. He asked if we wanted to ride with him to the store. When we arrived at the store, Dad sent me in to buy his cigarettes. He always bought Camels or Lucky Strikes. I didn't like buying cigarettes, even if it was for Dad. I was afraid people would think I was smoking them. I bought the cigarettes because I was told to do so.

When we returned home, Tony and I got out of the backseat of the car, and Tony shut the door. We had not noticed, however, that Dad's hand was on the mount between the front and the back door, and when Tony shut it, Dad's four fingers were crushed. I can't imagine how painful that must have been. Dad let out a scream of vulgarity, but that was the wrong move on his part because Tony and I ran away and had no intention of getting within arm's length of Dad, not with him screaming like a mad man. He finally realized he needed one of us to open the door for him to free his fingers. Somehow, he miraculously managed to get control of his filthy mouth and said, "Son, please open the door."

It took his saying please several times for us to decide we could get close enough to help him. We stayed out of his way for the rest of the evening. We found out later that one of his fingers was broken. Dad didn't go to the hospital because we did not have insurance. In the weeks and months to come, it was difficult for Dad to do his job as a TV repairman; he didn't have full use of his injured hand. Work started backing up at the shop, and Dad just drank more whiskey. I guess it was his way of dealing with the pressure of work and the pain from his injury.

PLUSES AND MINUSES

We moved from the shell house to a very old house about three miles from the Weiner city limits. Like the shell house, it also was located about a hundred yards off the main road down a dirt path. The house was in need of painting, and it reminded me of a house that would have been portrayed on TV as a haunted house. The only neighbors were located across the main road. Weeds had grown up in front of our house all the way to the main road. If you didn't know the house was there, you could easily drive right past it. Oh, how I missed the Blue House in Walnut Ridge, a place of security where I could hide from my world that was filled with insecurities at every turn.

Dad fell behind with his business rent, and I overheard

him telling Mother the landlord had asked him to move out. We were playing in the yard one Saturday morning when two men pulled up in the yard and took our car. I found out later it had been repossessed because we had not kept the payments up-to-date. We still had the delivery truck for the business, however, so we still had some transportation.

On September 15, 1961, we took Mother to the Jonesboro hospital to have the baby. Everything went well, and we had a new brother. We named him Byron Keith Simmons. I thought that was a fine name, and with the new addition, our family was blessed with three boys and one girl. Mom needed some help after having the baby, so as planned, Dad took us all to Grandmother and Grandpa Baird's house. We stayed only one week because Mother felt we needed to go home. I can only imagine what was going through her mind, worrying about our financial situation.

About mid-October, Tony and I was coming home on the school bus, and we saw Dad walking down the gravel road toward the house. The bus flew past him, but I was sure it was Dad. I wondered what was going on.

We arrived home, and shortly afterward, Dad came walking into the yard. He didn't say anything to us but headed straight into the house. I followed Dad in, it took me a while to figure out what had happened between all his ranting and raving and cursing. It seemed that someone had repossessed his truck at the TV shop and left him with no transportation. I remember Mother saying, "Freddie what are we going to do?" That question was asked many times during my childhood, and most of the time his answer was, "I don't know."

The business was locked up. Dad had no delivery truck, so he couldn't pick up or deliver TV sets. Losing his truck essentially put him out of business. Dad told Mother he had called his sister, Ruth Doyle, in Rockford, Illinois. Her husband, my uncle John Doyle, whom I really did not know that well, told Dad he could help get him a job in Rockford. Dad explained to Mother that he had already bought a one-way ticket. His plan was to go and look for work. He would be leaving for Illinois the next morning. The plan was for Dad to walk to the bus terminal in Weiner and use his one-way ticket to catch a bus to Rockford.

You get the picture: Dad was leaving town—and leaving Mother alone with four kids, along with the mess of the business Dad had started and abandoned. There were multiple TV sets locked up in Dad's shop with no way of returning them to the owners. There was rent owed on the business building and on the house in which we were living. Mother had very little money, hardly any food in the house, and four kids to care for. The only promise from Dad was that he would send money when and if he found work.

LIGHT IN THE DARKNESS

Dad left the next morning, and a month went by without word from him. Mother opened a charge account at a small corner grocery store in Weiner. I would ride my bike to the store and charge groceries from time to time.

The colder weather of November brought with it the need to have heat in the house. One day I had been playing outside, and as I came into the house I could smell a peculiar odor. Mother was hanging a blanket between the living room and the opening to the dining room. I asked her what that odor was.

"It's propane gas. We need to turn the stove in the living room down to a pilot light because we are running out of propane in the outside tank," she explained. "The pilot light will knock the chill out of the room, but from now on, we need to wear our coats in the house to stay warm. We need to save what little gas we have in the tank for cooking."

We all slept in one bed so we could stay warm. We had no heat in the bedroom, but the warmth from our bodies and the blankets kept us quite cozy throughout the night.

I knew Mother was scared after dark, and so was I, especially with no lights in the house after our electricity was shut off. Mom put chairs against the bedroom door to make it difficult for someone to break into our room while we slept. We kept a .22-caliber pistol on the nightstand by our bed. I have no doubt Mom would have used it to protect her family. Mother would light big candles when the darkness came. I never liked the candles because they caused our shadows to appear, and those shadows were always spooky to me.

Mother had a big Bible storybook like the one Mrs. Tompkins had read to us boys. I loved hearing Mother read those stories at night. It always soothed my mind and allowed me to think good thoughts about a loving God. I would review those stories in my mind over and over, finding comfort in a bad situation. I often asked questions, and Mother would answer them, always confirming that those stories were as real as we were.

THE PROMISE

Mom had faith, and so did I. It seemed to me that Mother's faith and hope in God grew stronger as times grew harder. As for me, I believed God knew everything that was happening in our lives, and He heard every prayer we prayed. I believed and was convinced in my heart that God loved us and was concerned about us; I pondered those thoughts over and over.

Our house was so cold, even during the day, that I would rather be outside than inside. I would often go to the field by the house, flatten an area of tall brown grass, and lie in it with my face to the heavens. The sun would heat the grass, and I would tuck my coat firmly up against my chin so the cold air could not get in. At last, I would find warmth.

I did a lot of thinking and talking to God during those times. You might call it praying, but I just called it talking to God about all kinds of things. I knew my mother was carrying a heavy burden, and I asked God to help her. Frequently at night, when Mother would read the Bible stories to us, I would see tears dripping down her cheeks. She was good at hiding those tears and would always put on a big smile, assuring us kids that everything would work out for the best. I believed her; I believed everything she said.

One evening after our story session, I walked over to Mom, hugged her neck, and whispered into her ear a promise that I have kept from that moment to this moment. I said, "Mother, don't you worry. I promise you that I will never drink." Mom knew I was saying that I would never drink alcohol. She hugged me tightly for a long time, probably wondering if a promise from a child could hold firm through the many years and life situations that were to come. I can confirm, however, that it has.

I am not opposed to others having an occasional drink, but because I saw how drinking alcohol negatively affected my dad—and, ultimately, my family—I made that promise and have kept it.

SCRAPS OF SACRIFICE

Mother was an amazing woman. There could be very little food in the house, but she still would cook up something tasty that filled our stomachs. One day when we sat down at the table, Mother had a cup of white beans called Great Northern beans. She also had fried some bread—it resembled pancakes, but it was fried bread. Mother dipped one spoonful of beans onto our plates, along with one piece of fried bread.

I said, "Mom, aren't you going to eat?"

"I've already eaten," she said.

"When did you eat?" I asked.

She said, "Eat your supper!"

I knew I hadn't seen her eat anything. After we kids finished eating, I walked into the kitchen and saw Mother eating the scraps from our plates. She sopped up the bean juice with the little pieces of fried bread that we'd left on our plates and ate them. I stepped back into the shadow of the door, not wanting Mother to know I saw her eating the scraps. The image of that moment will stay with me throughout eternity. I never want to forget that moment. I have reflected many times on Mother's sacrifices for her children and on the following scripture: "If we being evil know how to give good gifts to our children, how much more will our loving heavenly Father give to us" (Matthew 7:11 KJV).

THE LIST

One day Mom called me into the kitchen. "I need you to ride your bicycle into town and pick up some things at the corner store," she said. "Tell the man to put the items on our charge account." Mom made a list of a few items, and she told me to get myself a candy bar. She gave me specific instructions to eat it before I rode my bike back home.

I asked, "What about the other kids?"

She said, "They're not riding their bikes into town." She looked me straight in my eyes and said, "Do what I say." When Mother said for us to do what she said, that meant it was the end of the discussion.

It was a cold December day. It had been overcast all week. We had no way of knowing the weather forecast because we had no electricity in the house, and that meant no radio or television. It was about three miles to the city limits and another half mile or so to the store. I was a very athletic boy, and riding into town and back home was no big deal for me. I looked at it as an adventure and was glad to do something to help Mother. Mom gave me last-minute instructions about watching out for traffic and getting to the side of the road when a car was coming. It was amazing; that same bike I rode up and down Case Street in Jonesboro had become our only means of transportation. God had blessed me with that bike, and I had taken good care of His gift.

I shoved off, heading down the dirt path to the main

gravel road and toward the downtown area. About a mile down the road, I felt a drop of rain hit my face, and by the time I reached the city limits of Weiner, the rain had turned to sleet and was coming down hard. I didn't have a cap, and my hair was soaked by the time I got to the store. I didn't like going into the store with soaked hair and wet clothes—I was self-conscious enough about my appearance—but there was nothing I could do about the situation.

I parked my bike under the covering in front of the store. In those days, it never entered my mind that anyone would steal my bike; it was simply a different world. I guess things like that occurred elsewhere but not in our little town. I felt comfortable parking it on the sidewalk and just knew it would be there when I came back.

I went into the store, got a basket, and selected the items Mom had requested. I knew the layout of the store and where everything was located, and I was careful to get exactly what Mother had written down: a five-pound bag of sugar, a five-pound bag of flour, a large bag of Great Northern beans, one box of Lipton tea, one pound of bologna, and one loaf of light bread. You may think it strange that I remember the items on the list, but I have reviewed those items many times in my mind. Even today, some fifty-five years later, sometimes when I purchase one of those items I remember this incident that happened so long ago. I remember it with a thankful heart and with a "Thank you, Father" on my lips that I don't live that way anymore.

After collecting all Mother's items, I headed to the front of the store where the candy bars were displayed. I looked them over very carefully. I wanted one so badly, but I really wanted to get one for all of us. I knew that was out of the question, so after careful consideration, I picked the biggest one for the money—a Baby Ruth.

OUTSTANDING DEBT

I kept watching to make sure no one was at the checkout counter when I went forward with my items. I didn't want to ask for the items to be charged in front of other customers. I pulled my basket to the checkout, and the lady at the register was very nice as I took the items out of the basket. Then the owner of the store came over, and the lady moved behind him. It was obvious they had already discussed the situation. He immediately asked me how I was going to pay.

"Mother said to charge the items to our account," I answered. I looked behind me; another couple was standing in line to get checked out.

"I will charge these groceries," the owner said, "but no more until you pay your bill." I nodded my head to confirm I understood. He said, "Let's see what you have here, son." He rang up the sugar, flour, and tea and then said, "You don't need this light bread, do you?"

"I only picked up what Mother told me to buy."

He rang up the beans but put the lunch meat to the side by the bread. Then there was the candy bar. He chuckled and said, "One candy bar? Did she tell you to get one candy bar?"

I replied, "Yes, she did."

"I don't think you need a candy bar."

"Okay," I said.

Out of the corner of my eye, I could see several people

were now in line to check out. All I wanted to do was to get out of that store. He placed the groceries in a paper sack, and as he handed them to me, he repeated, "Tell your mother no more groceries until she pays her bill."

I nodded and headed for the door. I was so happy to be out of that store. I just wanted to go home!

For many years I felt badly toward that man for what he said and did that day. I don't think I would have handled that situation quite like he did, but years later, when I reflected on the incident, I concluded that he probably knew our family would never pay our bill. I decided he couldn't afford to feed everyone just because he ran a store. I realized he was obligated to pay for the items he was charging for us. In my resolve, I felt thankful for what he did for our family. Holding on to unresolved issues in our lives is like having outstanding debt. The sooner you settle your account, the better off you will be.

I went back to Weiner many years later with the intention of settling our account for whatever they felt we owed, but the store was long closed, and the building was empty. I bear no hard feelings toward that man, and I hope to meet him one day in heaven to thank him for the food he charged and ultimately gave to our family. God has a way of working out things like that. I trust that man and I will be friends one day and that he will be rewarded for the kindness he showed to my family.

CRUCIAL QUESTION

I got back on my bike, glad to be heading home. The sleet had turned to snow, and there was a light blanket of white on the road. I was glad that there was hardly any traffic. I remember thinking that the snow-covered streets were quite beautiful and much better than the icy rain that previously had soaked my clothes. I rode over the train tracks, holding the grocery sack with one hand and steering the bike with the other. The roads were slippery with the ice under the snow, and I knew I needed to be very careful. Down the paved street I rode, knowing the drop-off from the pavement to that dreaded gravel road that led to our house was fast approaching. As I rode from pavement to gravel, somehow my tire slid to one side. Even being as careful as I was, I lost control of my bike. Immediately I felt the cold, wet gravel against my face, and the paper sack—still held in one arm—ripped open, sending groceries sliding across that wet, snow-covered gravel road.

I saw the items from the sack flung across the road, and I started to get up, but for some reason, I lay my head back down on the gravel for a moment, and I asked God a question I will never forget. I said, "Lord, why do we have to live like this?" I wasn't mad with God. I just had that question in my mind and felt comfortable sharing it with God.

THE RIGHT IN THE WRONG

All that had happened that day, coupled with the things our family was dealing with, flashed through my mind. It just seemed like the right time and the right question, and I knew God was the right one to ask. I have never felt bad about asking God a question. There are times in our lives when we have questions because we don't understand something. There is a difference between asking God a question and questioning God. I believe God, in his love for us, wants us to have that kind of loving, close relationship with Him, a relationship in which we feel comfortable talking with Him about anything or everything going on in our lives. I believe this is what we are doing when we follow the Bible's instruction to pray without ceasing (1 Thessalonians 5:17 KJV).

Years later, I was thinking of the question I'd asked God that day, and the answer came to me. My family lived like that because we had a dad who was an alcoholic, and he didn't take care of his family. We may think our decisions in life don't affect anyone but ourselves, but the decisions we make always have an impact, either good or bad.

I picked up the items and put them between my shirt and coat and then stuffed the bottom of my coat into my blue jeans so they wouldn't fall out. I rode home thinking about the things I needed to tell Mom. When I got there, I told her what the man had said about no more credit.

She simply said, "Okay." Then she asked, "Did you eat the candy bar?"

I shook my head and showed her what I bought and told her what the store owner put back. I was not upset with not getting the candy bar. In a way, I was releaved because I felt bad knowing the other kids were not getting one. Mom dried me off and helped me out of my wet clothes. She hugged me close to her, and thanked me for riding my bike to the store in the cold and snow. Mothers have a way of making everything right in the world, and that's the way my mother made me feel at that moment.

3

Life Lessons: Pieces of Right and Wrong

As it is for Mike, your life is filled with a variety of choices—choices that can provide help when you need it. What are some of the choices before you today? Take time to write them down as you move through this section of study. These choices can add or take away from your life. Knowing the right thing to do is easy; actually doing the right thing is hard.

Shell House

What you see is not always what you want or need.

Mike's dad moved the family into a home that was incomplete. The outside may have looked good, but the inside still needed work. The property where the house was located looked firm, but after the first storm, the home became a swampy mess.

Have you ever made a quick decision without considering the consequences? In 1 Samuel 16:1–13, God directs the prophet Samuel to anoint a new king for Israel. God also told Samuel not to make a hasty decision. What decisions do you have to make? Is God prompting you to look past the obvious and wait? Maybe God is prompting you to move forward. On what are you waiting? If God is saying no, are you willing to follow His lead?

Different Day, Same Dad

*If you always do what you always have done,
you always will be what you always have been.*

Although Mike's dad changed locations with his family and business, he never made the needed change in his life. When he was accountable to a supervisor, there was no drinking on the job. As the owner of his new business, the boundaries that protected and preserved him and his family were no longer in place. Read Proverbs 25:28. When you can't lead yourself, you can't lead your family or a business. What are some areas in your life for which you need God to help set boundaries? Many people struggle with alcohol or other addictions. Do you have a quick temper or a foul mouth? If you do, ask God to help you change. Is there someone you trust with whom you can share your struggles so that person can help hold you accountable?

Pluses and Minuses

*A house and the heart have this in common:
they both can be filled with foolish items and ideas.*

Please read Psalm 37:25 and consider this: what was one satisfying moment in your life? Write it down, and explain why this means so much to you. What was one disappointing moment in your life? Do the same as above with this question.

Remember what was happening in Mike's life? His family had moved from a shell house to a broken-down home. Although it was closer to town and away from the swamp and mosquitoes, it was in desperate need of repair. One month after Mike's mom had a new baby, his dad left to find another job. Plus-and-minus experiences happened in Mike's life, and they happen in yours.

What do you do in these times? Have you ever been left with someone else's mess to clean up? How did you react? What comfort can you draw from the promise found in the Psalm above?

Light in Darkness

Even the smallest of lights can conquer
the greatest of darkness.

What can light do for you? For Mike, the pilot light in the family room stove brought warmth on a cold night. It also brought him a sense of protection in a dark night. To Mike, the light represented hope. How did the light bring hope? It allowed Mike's mom to read her big Bible storybook. The stories gave Mike hope and security during a frightening time in his life. Jesus's followers and Mary Magdalene experienced dark nights after Jesus was crucified. Read John 20:1–23, and think how God wants you to deal with your dark nights of fear or indecision. How can you turn you fears into trust?

The Promise

Before a promise is spoken with the mouth,
it should be guaranteed in the heart.

How do you hold on to a promise? Mike and his mother held on to a promise that enabled them to go through tough times. A promise can become sweeter the longer you wait for it, especially if the one making the promise is trustworthy. Was the promise from Mike's dad trustworthy? Why or why not? Was the promise made by Mike to his mother about never drinking alcohol trustworthy? Although time would show the security of that commitment, it was still a promise from a child who had yet to encounter adult temptations. What was the promise that helped Mike and his family endure every hardship? It was the promise they found in God's Word. Read Deuteronomy 31:8. There are many promises like this for needs in your life. Take the time to find one and hold on to it.

Scraps of Sacrifice

True sacrifice is willing to do without
so that others will not have to.

What would you be willing to give up for those you love? Would it be career, fame, fortune, or something as simple as food? Mike's memory of his mother eating scraps from the children's plates changed his life forever. In Romans 5:6–7, we read about God's willingness to sacrifice for us. How have you sacrificed for those you love? How have others sacrificed for you? How has the sacrifice of others, especially God, changed you?

The List

A list of groceries to cook and godly instructions
for life share this common trait: they both provide
the necessary ingredients for a meal of success.

In Deuteronomy 5:33, God promised a full life to His people, the Israelites. When you go shopping for someone, do you follow the list exactly? If you're like me, you come back with more than what's on the list. (That's why my wife doesn't send me anymore.) Mike followed the list that his mom gave him to the letter. He even got the candy bar that he was reluctant to get for himself. Why is it so important to learn obedience? It establishes the pattern in following God's instructions for a full and joyful life. Deuteronomy 5:33 teaches that obedience to God is honored and rewarded. What are some of the rewards you have experienced in your obedience to God?

Outstanding Debt

A man is never poorer than when he has bankrupted
his reputation and overdrawn his character.

At the checkout the other day, the cashier said to a customer, "Your card has been denied." The customer quickly pulled out another card and then another. The people behind grumbled while the customer became frustrated and embarrassed. What if that customer had been you? Mike encountered the embarrassment of not being able to pay. What do you think about the owner of the grocery store? What about the people standing behind Mike? What do you think about Mike's later change of heart toward the owner? Would you have reached the same conclusion? Would you have gone back years later to settle a debt owed? Read Mark 11:25, and compare it with Psalm 66:18.

Crucial Question

*The only true question is the one we ask when
we are truly willing to receive the answer.*

When we're young, we ask questions to help us understand our lives and the world around us. Later, we ask questions to learn at school, develop new skills, and to prepare for and advance our careers. Then there are the hard questions—the ones that keep us up at night and turn our stomachs. Lying on the cold road, looking up, Mike asked God, "Why?" Do you have questions like this in your life? Are you ready to ask them and to receive the answers? Psalm 57:1–3 is a powerful passage of prayer and praise that prepares a heart to receive the answers to the why questions in our lives. The question I have for you is this: Are you ready to receive the answer?

CHAPTER 4

Pieces of Mistakes and Miracles

LETTERS

On December 20, 1961, I went to the mailbox for Mother, and there was a letter from Dad. This was the first contact with him since he'd left for Rockford, looking for work. I ran back to our house from the main road, where our mailbox was located, and was so excited I could hardly breathe. I ran into the kitchen, waving the letter above my head and screaming to the other kids as I passed by them, "We have a letter from Dad!"

Mom grabbed the letter from my hand and headed to the living room, with all three of us kids on her heels. We all took a deep breath as Mom opened the letter. She started reading to herself at first, and then she paraphrased what Dad had written. He had found part-time work, and they would need him to work through Christmas. That's the part I remember the most—Dad would not be home for Christmas. We had never had a Christmas without the entire family together. I couldn't imagine Christmas without Dad, but a lot of things were going on in my life that I couldn't have imagined. I learned early in life that when there's nothing you can do about a situation, you should adjust and make the best of it. Mom held up a fifty-dollar bill and said, "Dad wants us to have a good Christmas."

We had not put up a Christmas tree because we didn't know how long we would be in our house. We thought, hoped, and prayed that Dad would pull up in the yard at any moment and move us to Rockford, where he had a job. We were just living from day to day, hoping for the best. Mother, a thirty-year-old woman with four children, was in the same desperate situation as we kids were in. We were all totally dependent upon Dad to rescue our family from this nightmare we were living. You may wonder how a woman gets herself into such a predicament, but it can happen quickly. By the grace of God, you may not be in a similar situation, but if you are, my heart goes out to you.

I hope you never judge the mistakes or situations in other people's lives, proclaiming, "I would never do that," or "I would never put up with that." The truth is, you don't know what you would do or how much you would put up with until the time comes, and you are faced with life's dilemmas. Many parents have lost daughters or sons because of stubborn pride. You may not agree with a decision your child has made, and you may have turned your back on him or her instead of opening your arms in love. God does not always agree with everything you do, but God never stops loving you. You should never stop loving and showing love to your children. You don't have to always agree to always love.

BERRIES AND POPCORN

After Mom assessed the situation, she got busy. I am sure if she could speak today, she would say she did it for her kids. She told Tony and me to cut a pine tree from the woods behind our house. We placed it in the living room. Mom popped popcorn, and we strung the kernels with a needle and thread. I picked some beautiful red berries from a tree in our yard, and we added them to the decorations. Mom brought out a box of plastic icicles, and we carefully positioned them on the tree. When we finished decorating, the tree was magnificent. We had created our own little masterpiece.

As I look back on that Christmas, I think about my sister, Cindy. She was six years old that year, the same age I was when we lived in the Blue House in Walnut Ridge. You might remember that when I was six, I didn't have a worry in the world; to me, life was perfect. I can't help wondering how different the world must have seemed for Cindy. It's amazing to me how God works in our lives by giving us the grace to cope with situations and circumstances as we assemble the pieces of our life puzzles.

I remember stringing the berries and popcorn and that Cindy was right in the middle of everything, lining up the articles for Tony and me to thread. I recall her laughter and how excited she was as we hung the ornaments on the tree. She was a child enjoying and savoring the wonderful moments of decorating for Christmas. Cindy was just a little girl, not thinking of whether we were rich or poor but only dreaming of the baby doll she hoped to receive on Christmas morning. How wonderful and precious are our little children.

A neighbor lady drove Mom into town to do some Christmas shopping. The gas company came on Christmas Eve. They put propane in our tank, giving us heat in the house and allowing Mom the ability to cook on Christmas Day. I never discussed this with Mom, but she must have used some of the money Dad sent to pay in advance for the propane.

LAUGHTER AND LOVE

On Christmas morning, our little feet hit the floor running. It was so nice to have a warm living room. Excitement soon filled our house when we realized we each had a present under the tree. There were gloves for me, which I loved because they were Rough Rider gloves with fringe down the side. Tony got a new book, probably science fiction, since that is what he enjoyed, and Cindy got her baby doll. We all gathered around Byron's crib for the unwrapping of his first Christmas present, a rattle, which was a big deal. Mom got handwritten notes and poems, hung on the tree and addressed "To Mother, with love," from each of us kids.

Mother cooked biscuits, and we had them with blackberry jam for breakfast. What a great Christmas! It had nothing to do with how much money was spent or how many gifts we received. It had everything to do with the laughter and the love we felt for each other. Mother told the story of the very first Christmas morning. We listened as she explained how the gift of baby Jesus changed the world forever. Mom was a great storyteller, and I loved listening to her stories over and over. On Christmas morning 1961, Mother took the time to make everything right in our little world.

Family Meal

Uncle Carl and Aunt Betty came to our house for an unexpected visit on the day after Christmas. We had not seen them since our move to Weiner. We had no phone and no electricity in our house. To say they were shocked by our living conditions would be an understatement. Uncle Carl was Mother's younger brother, a man I admired very much then and admire even more today. Carl was twenty-five years old then, and Aunt Betty was twenty-four. They had two children: Carl Jr., who at that time was five years old, and Sherry, who was four. Carl worked for Frolic Footwear, where they made shoes. He was a leather cutter, which was considered a good job for factory work, and it provided a good living for his family.

Mother explained our situation to them, and I could tell they recognized the concern in her voice as she told our story. They didn't stay long, but they asked Mother if they could come for all of us on Friday evening and take us to their house for the weekend. Mother agreed, and I will be eternally grateful for what Carl and Betty did for our family. They not only picked us up on that Friday, but for the next several months they took our family to their home in Jonesboro. Always on the trip back to Weiner, Uncle Carl would stop at a local grocery store, where he paid for enough groceries to feed us for the next week.

Mother picked out things like a giant bag of Great Northern beans, a ten-lb bag of potatoes, 5lb sack of sugar, and flour. We rarely had meat, but sometimes the store had hamburger meat on sale at five pounds for a dollar. Mom would buy the hamburger meat and make spaghetti. We had homemade cornbread with almost every meal. (Oh, how I would love some of Mom's cooking today.) She could take little and make it into a wonderful, filling meal. Mom knew how to cook a meal that would keep our stomachs full.

SMALL ACTS, GREAT IMPACTS

I will never forget what Carl and Betty did for our family and their kindness to us. They were so young, with a family of their own, yet they came faithfully every Friday afternoon. Betty loved to cook tacos, and we loved to eat them! They were homemade with fresh ingredients. She prepared them every Friday night, and oh, how I looked forward to Friday nights and Aunt Betty's tacos.

Betty has now gone to be with the Lord, but I still visit my Uncle Carl whenever I get back to Arkansas. Sometimes when it is just him and me, I will thank him for what they did for our family. With humility, he will laugh and say something funny, such as, "You all surely ate a lot of potatoes." I love Uncle Carl, who is now eighty years young, and I love Aunt Betty. I want to be there at the judgment seat of Christ in heaven when they receive their reward for the kindness and love they showed to our family in great need.

Who would have thought that a ten-year-old boy in 1961 would remember and be eternally grateful for their kindness over fifty-five years later. The truth is whether people remember your kindness or not, God does not forget anything. He will remember small bits or large chunks of kindness at the judgment seat of Christ, and your account will be settled for the way you have lived your life.

Some people will be rewarded, and some will lose rewards, depending upon the motive of their hearts. My suggestion is to never pass up an opportunity to do a kind deed for your neighbor. Who is your neighbor? It's anyone God puts in your path during your life on this earth. Life is short compared to eternity. It has been said—and I agree—that the only thing we can take into eternity with us is the kindness and generosity we give away in this life.

ENOUGH

A certain man lived in a small town in Georgia. He owned a textile mill. This man was probably in his eighties. He employed around a hundred people at his mill. One day the mill caught fire and burned to the ground. As the TV crews stood in front of the rubble, they asked the owner if he had insurance; he did. They followed up with the question, "What are you going to do now that your mill has burned down?"

He replied, "I will build it back."

The reporter quickly asked, "Why would you do that? Textile mills are going out of business every day."

"All my employees depend on me for employment," the old man explained.

The young reporter countered by saying, "You could take the insurance money and live a very comfortable life."

The old man then replied with a profound statement that I have never forgotten. He said, "A man can only wear so many suits and eat so many steaks."

That is so true. When is enough, enough? I believe the world would be a much better place to live if we all thought more like this wise older gentleman.

LITTLE THINGS, BIG LESSONS

One weekend when we were at Uncle Carl's house, Mother called my aunt Ruth—Dad's sister—in Rockford, Illinois, and asked to speak with Dad. Ruth explained that Dad had gone back to Arkansas because he hadn't found full-time work in Rockford. Ruth said he was at their mother and dad's house in Dixie. Mom called their home, and Grandpa Simmons answered the phone. Mother explained to him the whole fiasco up to this point.

Grandpa told Mother that Dad was working with my uncle Riley at Riley's sawmill in Dixie, Arkansas. He said he would have Dad move us to Dixie as soon as they could find a suitable house.

I loved Grandmother and Grandpa Simmons! Grandpa Simmons was probably one of the kindest men I have ever known. With Grandpa being true to his word, a few days later Dad pulled up into our yard in a huge logging truck. I think we kids were more excited to see him than he was to see us. He was in a big hurry to get the truck loaded with our furniture and get out of town. I asked Mother about that several years later, and she told me he hadn't wanted people in town to know he was back because he owed money to so many of them.

We worked hard loading that truck with every piece of furniture we owned. Dad put the sideboards on the logging truck, and we left town as soon as we could. Tony and I rode in the back of the truck with the furniture. It was mid-March, so it was still cool riding in the open air. I remember thinking as we drove away, *This house hasn't been a pleasant place to live.*

I understand now that although it might not have been pleasant, it was an important piece in my life puzzle. I've remembered the days of playing in the yard and warming myself as I lay in the tall brown grass, surveying the clouds in the beautiful blue sky. I did a lot of wondering, thinking, and planning on those days, covering all sorts of issues. These are good memories of times that helped shape my life as I grew up and made me thankful for what we had. I learned not to take little things for granted.

As we drove through town I saw Dad's TV repair sign still hanging on the front of the rented TV shop. Only a few months earlier we all had such high hopes for a wonderful life as Dad started his own business. I learned early in life that things don't always work out as planned. We hit the highway, and I saw the corner store where I'd charged groceries for our family. We zoomed right on by, with no thought of paying off our grocery bill. This was just another example of how to become a deadbeat and not pay people for what they were owed. I hated that about our family, but it all rolled back to our dad and the examples he set for us kids. I hate making statements like that because it seems like I'm coming down hard on my dad. Everything he was I made a mental note *not* to be. That is so sad because I always loved my dad. I just never wanted to be like him.

MIRACLE

Grandpa Simmons was responsible for renting our family the little house in Dixie. I was grateful for what he did, even if it meant changing schools again. Moving from Weiner was a blessing for Mother and us kids. I know working at Uncle Riley's sawmill was hard work. Fortunately, Dad was a young man, and if he stayed off the liquor, everything could work out for our family. Many a day I worried about Dad because I knew the sawmill could be a very dangerous place to work—accidents could happen so quickly. Some of the men working with Dad had missing fingers or, worse, a missing hand, and the workers didn't mind sharing their stories

We didn't own a vehicle; they all had been repossessed in Weiner. Everywhere our family went, we drove the big logging truck from Uncle Riley's business. It was an eyesore but served its purpose of getting our family from point A to point B. One day my aunt Charcie—Riley's wife and Dad's sister—invited our family to their house for a fish fry. I was excited because I knew there would be lots of kids my age to play with. We drove to their house in the logging truck. We were all sitting in the front seat—five of us, plus our baby brother Byron, whom Mother was holding. As we drove up, Dad parked on an incline at the side of the house. I'm not sure how it happened, but as Dad came to what I thought was a stop, I opened the passenger door, and somehow I tumbled from the front seat to the ground—it all happened so fast. My legs were stretched out on the ground when Dad clutched the truck, taking it out of gear and allowing it to immediately roll back.

I watched the huge truck tire roll over my right ankle—I can still see it in my mind's eye. There was no pain. I saw the tire roll over me like I was a speed bump in the road but without pain and without injury. Mom was at my side very quickly and helped me up. I told her what had happened, but she told me to be quiet.

"That couldn't have happened," she said, "or your foot would be crushed."

I again insisted that the truck had rolled over my ankle.

This time Mom popped me on my head. "Shut up," she told me. "People will think you're crazy for saying something like that."

Dad came around to check on me, but I kept my mouth shut. I knew if Mother didn't believe what had happened, Dad would certainly not believe my story. I brushed off my jeans, and as I ran out to the front yard to play with the other boys, I simply said, "Lord, thank you for not letting my foot get crushed." I did not speak of that incident to anyone for many years, except to God Himself. I knew what happened, and so did God. I was grateful for the miracle He performed for me on that day. I have always been thankful and have expressed my gratitude to God many times, as a boy and as an adult.

Years later, when I was in my late twenties, I was talking to Mother, and I brought up that incident. I asked her if she remembered that day and what had happened. She remembered, but she asked if I would tell her the story again. I told her exactly what had happened, and Mother said she believed me. It meant a lot to me that she believed my story after all those years because I knew it was true. Here is the way I see things: whether Mom believed me or not, God and I know what happened, and that has been good enough for me. Today, through this book, He is letting me share this miracle with you and the world, I can't help but think what a wonderful and great God we serve. God loves to work miracles in our lives. All we need to do is open our eyes and believe.

I plan on discussing this miracle with God, face-to-face, one day, as well as several other miracles that have happened in my life. I have said "Thank you, Lord" many times, but I want to tell Him how grateful I am for what He did for me on that day. If there was a guardian angel involved, and I believe there was, I want to shake his hand and say with a big smile, "Well done! You honored our Lord by doing your assigned job, and you took good care of me." Who knows? He may have many more stories to tell me about my life of which I am not aware. How intriguing!

DIXIE

I enjoyed living in Dixie. Our house was located a short walk from the banks of the Saint Francis River, a swift-running river that emptied into the muddy Mississippi River. As a boy, I spent many of my Saturdays fishing the Saint Francis. Mom would pack me a lunch and a jug of water, and I would leave home early in the morning, not to return until late in the evening.

Most of the time I was alone on the riverbank, but I didn't mind. I liked being alone, with nothing but the open sky above me, my fishing pole, and a can of red worms for bait.

I usually fished for catfish, and I loved the thrill of fishing in the swift current of the river. Although I had not been to church since we left Jonesboro, where I attended the Church of the Nazarene, I would spend my days on the riverbank, mentally reviewing Bible stories and the words the preacher spoke of God's love for His children. I considered myself a child of God and often referred to God as my heavenly Father. I always felt comfortable going to God. Some would say it was in prayer, but I would call it just talking.

As an adult, I love to take my four-mile daily walk around Walden Lake here in Plant City, Florida. As I walk, I enjoy talking privately with God about everything going on in my life. I love to start by remembering, with thanksgiving, all that God has done for me. He has truly opened the windows of heaven and poured out blessings I can hardly contain. I want God to remember me as being a thankful man, a man who returns to Him to say thank you. I am reminded of a story in the Bible in which Jesus healed ten men, but only one returned to say thank you. Jesus asked, "Were there not ten cleansed? But where are the nine?"

MOUSE

Dad was making good money working at the sawmill. We had a nice little house and food on the table. Things were getting back to normal, and I was beginning to feel a little more secure about my life. Dad was not drinking—at least, not that I knew of—and Mother seemed happier than she had been in months.

School had dismissed for the summer, and I was glad. We

moved so much, I should have been accustomed to making friends quickly, but nothing could be further from the truth. I was not an outgoing little boy. The only thing I had going for me was my athletic ability. I loved playing ball—any kind of ball; it really didn't matter. I didn't make very many friends during the short time I attended school at Dixie. I was so quiet that my family nicked named me "Mouse." I always hated that name, but I never acted like it bothered me. If you remember, I was always the one talking and asking questions, especially when we lived in the Blue House. Not anymore; the last five years had changed my perspective on life. I felt unsure of myself, like I had nothing to contribute to any conversation; at least, nothing anyone would be interested to hear.

It is amazing how quickly a little boy's personality can change. I'm thankful that through those years, I held firmly to my faith in God. I believed with all my heart that God loved me and that His eyes were always upon me. I don't know what would have happened to me in my young life if it had not been for the Church of the Nazarene and the people who invested their time to introduce me to my heavenly Father. It was the only stability I had in my life.

PREPARATION FOR LIFE

Midsummer came, and Dad arrived home with bad news. The sawmill had gone bankrupt and would be closing in a few weeks. Dad talked to some people about interviewing for a job on Potters' farm. This farm was located off Owl City Road near a small town named Hoxie. It looked like, once again, we would be moving to a new school district in the fall. I had no way of knowing what this new move would bring. I didn't know that over the next few years, I would be faced with the most trying events of my young life.

I am grateful for the time in Dixie when it was just God and me, fishing from the banks of the Saint Francis River. Our conversations turned out to be precious gifts from above. It allowed time for God to prepare my young mind for what was coming and for the grace I would need to survive.

It has been said that it is a blessing from God to live out our lives by faith, not knowing what the next pieces of our life puzzles will look like. I believe God uses people, places, and things to prepare us for future events and the work He has predestined us to do. God saves us for a purpose, and the happy moments as well as the trials and heartache of our lives serve as learning pieces to our life puzzles. As we live and carefully place each piece, we are preparing ourselves for future service. These are all life lessons to be used today or possibly twenty years in the future.

4

Life Lessons: Pieces of Mistakes and Miracles

When you are putting a puzzle together, especially one with hundreds of pieces, some pieces always seem not to fit anywhere. You wish you could toss them away. In our lives, we also have pieces that we wish we could do without, but those moments of frustration could become a miracle in the making. Maybe, as time passes, we will see a bigger picture and will be able to move forward to complete the puzzle. In chapter 4, Mike provided a reminder that we have positive and negative experiences in our lives. If you try to avoid or forget a particular experience, you may end up with more than a hole in your puzzle; you might experience an unfinished life.

Letters

The difference between a postcard and a
letter is that a postcard enters your mailbox
while a letter enters your heart.

Decisions were put on hold for Mike and his family because of questions and uncertainties they faced in Weiner, Arkansas. That changed when Mike's dad sent a letter with money in it. Would you have received the letter with anticipation or anger? Are you in a situation of waiting in uncertainty because of someone else? Do you tend to judge others who are in this type of situation? Proverbs 25:11 tells us, "Like apples of gold in settings of silver is a word spoken in right circumstances." How can you encourage someone in this type of situation?

Berries and Popcorn

Popcorn is strung together with thread.
Memories are strung together with love.

Do you have childhood memories of decorating a Christmas tree? What was your favorite part? Did you have a specific job? That year, Mike saw Christmas as more than getting gifts. He was thinking about his younger sister, Cindy, who was as excited about Christmas as Mike had been at that age. The great missionary Paul reminds us of the right perspective for our thoughts. He writes, "Finally, brothers and sisters, whatever is true, whatever is noble, whatever is right, whatever is pure, whatever is lovely, whatever is admirable—if anything is excellent or praiseworthy—think about such things" (Philippians 4:8). Cindy dreamed of future gifts, while Mike fondly remembered the past. Which do you think of? Why?

Laughter and Love

If love and laughter were the only presents under
the Christmas tree, would it be enough?

I heard a story about a boy whose Sunday school teacher asked him to define kindness. The boy said, "It is when my mom makes me biscuits for breakfast."

His teacher then asked, "Can you tell me what loving kindness is?"

He thought for a moment and then replied, "Oh, that is when she puts jam on them for me."

Mike's mom made a special breakfast for the kids on Christmas. We might not have called it a feast, but the kids thought it was. Consider this thought: "Better is a dish of vegetables where love is than a fattened ox served with hatred" (Proverbs 17:1). How does it apply to Mike and his family? How does it apply to you?

Family Meal

An ordinary meal made by hands can feed you for a day.
A family meal made from the heart
can feed you for a lifetime.

Uncle Carl and Aunt Betty became involved with Mike and his family. Write down some of the positive attributes and actions they exhibited to help take care of Mike and his family. How have you been "fed for a lifetime" by someone's actions? How have you fed others in the same way? What does Proverbs 11:25 mean when it says, "A generous person will prosper, and anyone who gives water will receive a flood in return." How do you think God blessed Carl and Betty for their generosity? How will God bless you for your generosity?

Small Acts, Great Impacts

The greatest of dreams considered will never
match the smallest of deeds completed.

Carl and Betty taught Mike more than just a routine of
weekend trips and tacos. They taught him how to give
graciously, even when you may not have much to spare.
In Matthew 10:42, we read, "And if you give even a cup
of cold water to one of the least of my followers, you will
surely be rewarded." How have you demonstrated this to
a member of your family? How about a stranger? What
did Jesus mean by the reward? Mike also was taught how
to be grateful for what he had been given. Take the time
to read Matthew 25:31–46. How does the Lord show His
gratitude for your willingness to serve others?

Enough

*It does not matter how much wood you put on a
fire. The flames will always say, "Never enough!"*

When the textile mill owner was asked what he would do
after the fire, his response was, "Build it back." How do
you think today's world would react to his answer? What
would you have told him to do? Why? Jesus warned against
selfishness in Luke 12:16–34. The mill owner decided to
rebuild the mill. What do you think the true "treasure" of his
heart was? Would you have the same treasure?

Little Things, Big Lessons

*What you do announces who you are better
than any words you can ever speak.*

How fast can you load a truck with furniture? That depends
on a lot of things: weather, the amount of furniture, the size
of the truck, and if you owe people money. Mike had two
memories during the move. The first was of the old house
he was leaving behind. What were some of the little things
that he enjoyed? Mike also saw his dad's closed shop and the
corner store where they owed money. What was a big lesson
that Mike took away from that experience? What was the
impact of his dad's bad example? Ephesians 6:2 reminds us,
"Honor your father and mother." Can we do this but still not
approve of what they do? How would you have responded in
this situation? Why?

Miracle

One does not have to see miracles to know they happen.

The logging truck rolled over Mike's ankle yet did not injure him. Do you believe in miracles? Have you experienced one? Did others believe you? It's interesting that Mike's dad's finger was broken after being slammed in the car door, yet Mike's foot was uninjured after being run over by a one-ton vehicle. What do Psalm 91:11 and Luke 4:10 have in common with this part of Mike's life?

Dixie

True prayer begins with the openness of the
heart before the opening of the mouth.

Where do you go for prayer? When Mike moved to Dixie, Arkansas, he found a place to be alone with God. Now in his senior years, he still has a routine of spending time with God around a local lake. Do you have such a time and place? Luke 5:16 tells us, "Jesus often withdrew to lonely places and prayed." Do your prayers consist of lists for God or of listening to God? In Luke 17:11–19, ten men received healing from Jesus—a miracle! Yet only one came back to give thanks. How can this passage change your view of prayer?

Mouse

Regarding confidence, one cannot roar like
a lion with the heart of a mouse.

Mike felt that he could not contribute to conversations. Have you ever felt that way? What or who made you silent in your life? Mike wasn't always this way, but what changed him? Read Romans 8:26–39. If you lost your voice, can you find it again? How can you help others find their voices?

Preparation

Consistency and continuity are found only in the Creator,
not the created.

Throughout this chapter, Mike described both mistakes and miracles. How did these situations improve his character? How can circumstances like these develop your character? Hebrews 13:5–8 provides you a promise of consistency from God. How can you apply this to your life when surrounded by inconsistent people and circumstances?

CHAPTER 5

Pieces of Trauma and Trust

ANOTHER ADVENTURE

Dad left home one Saturday morning to interview for the job at Potters' farm. I hoped that Dad would be home by noon with the good news of a job ... but that wasn't the way it turned out. He didn't come home until after dark, and he was slurring his words. This was the first time I knew of his drinking since we had moved to Dixie. I'd hoped those days were behind us and that Dad would keep steady work so he could provide for our family. It was moments like these when I thought back to a happier time when we lived in the Blue House, a time when I felt a sense of stability. I just wanted things to be like they used to be.

Mother was aggravated with Dad, but as he came into the house, he declared, "I just stopped by the tavern to have a beer; there's nothing wrong with that!" Mom was disappointed because there was no such thing as Dad having just one beer. We all remembered what life had been like when he was drinking on a regular basis, and none of us wanted to go back to that way of life.

The next morning we found out Dad had gotten the job. He explained that we would be moving to R. L. Potters' farm, located on the outskirts of Hoxie. I hated to move again, not because I had a lot of friends in Dixie but because we lived close to my grandparents, and I loved spending the night with them. There was a small country church located not far from their house. I thought maybe we could start attending services there. Unfortunately, my aspirations of attending the country church never worked out.

Uncle Riley still owned the big logging truck, and he and Dad used it to move our family to Potters' farm. Dad bought a green Buick for $150, giving us a means of transportation. Mother drove the car behind the logging truck to our new home.

It seems that wherever we lived, the houses were located off the main road. This time we turned off the main gravel road onto another private lane that was about half a mile back to a small house, surrounded by soybean and rice fields. Tractors were parked near some working sheds, but my main interest was the house. As soon as we parked, I took off running to scout it out, hoping the inside was better than the outside. Unfortunately, that was not the case.

I made a quick walk through the house, looking for the bathroom, I soon found out there wasn't one. There were three bedrooms, a living room, and a kitchen. The living room had a wood-burning pot-bellied stove. It was in the middle of the room and was used primarily for heating the living room and kitchen areas. There was no running water and, as I mentioned, no indoor bathroom; there was, however, an outhouse located about twenty yards from the back porch. At this point we were all very quiet. No one complained, because we knew Dad would come down hard on anyone who was negative. The house came with the job, as part of Dad's weekly salary, so there was no rent to pay, and that was a blessing. There was a hand pump in the front yard and a bucket with a dipper in the kitchen to store water for drinking and cooking. Mom was happy because there was a gas stove in the kitchen. I spotted a number 2 washtub hanging from a nail located on the back porch, and Mom explained it was for bathing. We all laughed because Mom was kind of chubby. We tried to get her to sit in the washtub to see if she could fit. We all had a good chuckle, especially Mother, and we accepted our new lifestyle as another adventure.

STEPPING UP

School was out for the summer, and as soon as I could, I started scouting out the farm. There were no rivers to fish, like I had in Dixie, but the rice canals were loaded with fish. There was a big mound of black dirt at the back of the farm. I asked some of the hired workers if they knew why the soil was so dark, and they explained it was where an Indian mound was located. They explained that arrowheads and pieces of Indian pottery could be found in the mound. That's all I needed to know. I started searching the mound and, in time, found some beautiful arrowheads and some spearheads. I saved them and still have my collection today.

Friday was payday for Dad, so that was when we usually

went to town to buy groceries. One day while in the grocery store, a man walked up to Mother and said, "Kathleen, how are you?" It was Bill Howard, my Sunday school teacher from Jonesboro, Arkansas. I didn't know it, but Mother and he had gone to high school together. What a small world. Most people would say it was a coincidence, but I don't believe in coincidences. God has a plan for our lives, and He places people where He needs them in order to accomplish His overall will.

Bill Howard explained to Mom that he had started a home mission Nazarene church in Walnut Ridge, a town two miles from Hoxie. He was serving as the pastor. He invited us to church, but Mother told him that we lived too far out in the country and that my dad would never agree to drive that distance to attend church on Sundays. Bill asked where we lived, and when Mom told him, he said he would pick us up if we wanted to attend church.

Thank God for Christian people who are willing to serve others. I was overjoyed. I couldn't believe my ears. We were going to be back in church and with a godly man I admired. I wanted so badly to be in church, and God worked it out on a Friday afternoon in, of all places, a supermarket. I thank God that He never forgets about His children. When we least expect it, God hands us a miracle. God answered the prayers of a twelve-year-old boy living at the back side of nowhere.

Bill Howard was true to his word, and for the next two years, until we moved, he picked us up and took us to church. Mother attended church with us kids for a while, but Dad caused problems, and soon just Tony and I attended. Mother never mentioned why she quit going, but I got the impression that Dad was a little jealous of the pastor, Bill Howard. To keep friction down, Mom stopped going, but she always made sure we were ready when the car pulled up on Sunday morning.

LATE NIGHT SHOW

Over the next two years, Dad started drinking heavily. I mentioned he was paid on Friday evenings, and sometimes he wouldn't come home until one or two o'clock Saturday morning. This didn't happen every Friday, but usually once or twice a month he would stay out drinking all night. It was nothing for him to miss the driveway when he arrived home and run the car through the fence in our front yard. He would then proceed to tear the house apart, breaking dishes and wreaking havoc. He always wanted to fight with Mother, and, unfortunately, he liked an audience; namely, us kids. He would wake everyone and gather us in the living room for the show.

As time progressed, he became more and more abusive. He would get Mother down on the floor and hold a knife to her throat, telling us he was going to kill her. I saw him beat her in the head with a hard-handled hunting knife and bruise her all over her forehead. I saw him hold Mother's face inches from the red-hot pot-bellied stove in the living room, telling her he would burn off the side of her face so no other man would ever want her. I would double up my fists and tear into him, telling him to leave Mother alone. He would throw me across the room, and I would bounce off the wall and charge at him again.

One day before Dad got home, Mother got Tony, Cindy, and me together and told us that the more we fought and begged Dad to stop, the more abusive he became. She asked us to try to ignore him, and maybe he would stop. That was hard to do. We tried, but it didn't work.

On several occasions, Dad got out his shotgun. He would load it in front of all the family and as he loaded it, he would explain how he was planning to kill everyone. He would name our names in the order he planned to kill us. He would hold the shotgun to Mother's head and tell us kids, "Say good-bye to your mother!"

ZIGZAGGING

One Saturday afternoon Dad was drinking whiskey from a bottle wrapped in a brown paper bag. He left the room but came back with his shotgun. This time he told us he was going to kill himself—quite a change. He loaded the gun and said good-bye to us, explaining that he didn't deserve to live. He walked out on the front porch, and as the shotgun blast resounded through the air, we heard his body fall to the wooden porch floor. There was total silence for several minutes and then Cindy said to Mother, "Dad has killed himself."

Mother said, "No, he hasn't. Just be quiet." In a few minutes, we heard scratching on the screen door. Mom was correct; he was very much alive.

Dad opened the door and found us all sitting on the couch. He said, "Not one of you came out to check on me.

I could have been bleeding to death out there. Because you didn't check on me, I am going to kill you all."

At that moment, I sprang from the couch and told him I was going to a neighbor's house to call the police. I said, "I am going to tell everything you have done to our family."

Dad said, "If you go, I will kill them all. When you get back, we will all be dead."

"You've already said your plan was to kill us all," I said, "so what difference does it make?" I ran out the front door and through the gate. As I ran past the car—*bam!*—a shotgun blast rang out, and the side of the car folded up like a tin can. I kept running but started zigzagging as I ran down the road. I thought, *He may shoot me, but I'm not going to make it easy for him.*

I left the road as soon as I could and ran into a rice field. I found myself hunkered down in a squatting position. In a few minutes, I saw our car very slowly driving down the road past where I was hiding. Dad was driving, and his shotgun was hanging out the window. As he approached me, I heard him say, "Mike, come out. I'm not going to hurt you. Come out, and we'll go to Dixie this afternoon to visit Grandmother and Grandpa Simmons." He knew how much I loved them, and if anything would entice me to come out, that would.

I held my breath because I didn't want to move the rice heads, which would be a sure giveaway of my location. I squatted as low as I could, and that's when I felt the water, which was about a foot deep in the rice field, as it wet the seat of my jeans. Not breathing, I didn't raise up. I stayed in place as Dad drove by several more times and then drove back to the front yard, where he parked the car and went into the house. In about thirty minutes, Mother walked out to the area where I was hiding and called my name. I came out, and she told me Dad had lain across the bed and was asleep.

PROTECT US

I told Mother a few days later that if Dad ever threatened to kill her again, I was going to shoot him. She said, "Don't say that. You would go to jail, and it would ruin your whole life."

I knew Mother was right, so, in my resolve, I asked, "What are we supposed to do? Wait until he kills one of us, either on purpose or by accident? Either way, we will be just as dead."

That was always my big fear—that he would kill Mom and we kids would be scattered in foster homes all over the state, separated from each other for the rest of our lives. It is awful for a boy to feel that way about his dad. I didn't hate him. I was just afraid he would make a mistake someday and accidently kill one of us.

You may have lived through times that were as bad or worse than what I experienced. I was blessed because I had a sweet mother, a good church, and a good pastor who preached God's Word every Sunday. I started praying that God would protect us during these times. Our mother was a good woman. She was a Christian who only knew a little about the scriptures, but it was enough to satisfy the questions from a twelve-year-old boy. With every episode Dad starred in, I thought about my promise to Mother not to drink. I was more determined than ever to keep that promise.

THE COACH

I loved playing ball, and as it turned out, Hoxie had a basketball team. I was in the sixth grade that year, and Mr. Dalson was the coach. We practiced at school, and I loved every practice. When it came time to start the season, Mr. Dalson placed me as the center. I knew all along that I would not be able to play because there was no way Dad would bring me into town for a ball game. I told the coach my situation, and he offered to pick me up and bring me home after the games. I wanted to play, but I didn't want him to see where we lived. I agreed to meet him on the main road about half a mile from our house.

On the night of the first game, I walked out to the main road where we kids caught the school bus. As promised, Coach Dalson picked me up and brought me home after the game. I told him he could let me out on the main road, and I would walk the rest of the way home. I really didn't want to walk home because it was dark, and the road home was long and scary for a young boy with a wild imagination.

Mr. Dalson told me he would drive me to my front door, so away we went, with me still feeling embarrassed over the condition of our house. We pulled up in front, and I thanked him for the ride and watched him drive away. To my surprise, the world had not come to an end. He had not made any negative comments about our house. It wasn't a big deal to anyone but me. From then on, he picked me up at the house and brought me home, and I learned a valuable lesson. People are much more concerned about the kind of person you are than the kind of house you live in.

GOD'S WAYS

That year, basketball was a big part of my life, and we didn't lose a single game. I made lifelong friends at Hoxie, and I attribute that, at least in part, to my ability to play ball. I have thought many times about the truck that could have crushed my foot and prevented me from ever playing ball or perhaps leaving me with a limp for the rest of my life. It is with a grateful heart that I give thanks to God.

You may ask why God would do that for me and not do the same for your cousin Vinnie or your uncle Joe. I don't have that answer. God's ways are higher, and His thoughts are greater than mine or yours. God extends mercy to whomever He chooses for whatever reasons he declares. Remember that to try to explain God and everything He does would be like trying to pour the ocean into a child's beach bucket; it can't be done. I am thankful for the blessings He extends to me, and I am certain you have many blessings for which you can thank Him also.

RAY OF SUNLIGHT

One day I came home from school and knew something was wrong because Dad was already home, bathed, and cleaned up. As we gathered in the living room, Dad broke the news: our grandpa Simmons had passed away that morning. I was heartbroken because I loved him so much. Dad explained that we were going to the town where they lived, Paragould. We would be there for a few days for the funeral. I had never attended a funeral and wasn't sure what that would entail.

When we got to their house and went in, everything was quiet. I saw Grandmother Simmons sitting in the living room. I hugged her and began to cry. After we got settled, Grandmother told the story of how Grandpa had died.

"I went into the bedroom where your grandpa was and asked if he could eat some breakfast. He said yes, so I went back into the kitchen to cook him an egg with bacon and toast," she said. "When I came back into the room to tell him breakfast was ready, I noticed he had not gotten up. There was a ray of sunlight shining through the window where I had previously opened the curtain, and it was shining on the foot of the bed, right on your grandpa's feet. I said, 'Fred,' but he didn't answer me. I saw a cigarette was still between his fingers, half burned down. I called his name again and touched him, but I knew that he was gone."

Grandmother said, "I just sat down in the chair beside the bed and talked to God. I told Him how grateful I was that your grandpa Fred didn't suffer. I knew he had not suffered because the lit cigarette was still between his fingers." She looked at me, knowing that I loved him so much, and said, "Mike, it is as though an angel came down from heaven on that ray of sunlight just to pick up your grandpa to take him home."

I knew my grandparents were Christians, but they didn't talk much about their beliefs. I wish they had, and I wish Grandpa would have shared his love for God with me before he died. I wish he had shared with me some Christian stories about his life so I could write about them today. I truly believe the greatest gift we can give to our children or grandchildren is our faith in Jesus. Our children need to hear what God has done for us so they can make their decisions for Christ early in their lives. I hope my son, Steve, and my grandchildren will remember my love for God and, through the stories of my life puzzle, will learn to love and trust God as I do. I know I will see Grandpa again in heaven someday. What a wonderful hope Christian people have, that someday they will be reunited with their loved ones, never to be separated again.

BONO HILL

We lived at Potters' farm for two years, and then our family moved to a house on Bono Hill. The little town called Bono was located between Walnut Ridge and Jonesboro. Dad got a job driving a propane truck, delivering propane gas to residents, primarily in rural areas. I really hated to leave Hoxie because for the first time I had made many friends at school. Playing basketball did open the door for me to make good friends and to feel at least somewhat secure. I knew I would miss going to church too. I loved the Nazarene church, and I loved Bill Howard, our pastor. We told him where we were moving, and he promised he would check on us from time to time. I was glad because I'd been afraid I would never see him again.

We moved to a little brick-siding house on Bono Hill. It was named that because after you left the town of Bono, you would come to a big hill on the main highway (US 63), and we lived at the top of that hill. Everyone just called it Bono Hill, and that identified where we lived. We always hoped that our lives would get better with each move, but that really wasn't the case. Dad cooled down his drinking for a while, but it didn't last long.

One night Dad arrived home and obviously had been drinking heavily. He did his usual routine of wreaking havoc on the family. Somehow during his escapades, he fell down into a steep gully that was located by the main gravel road. At the bottom of the gully was a small lake. We could hear him yelling for help. He was screaming, "Help me! I'm drowning!" It was a moonless night and very dark. Mother was concerned that he would fall into the lake and drown. She and I got into the car, drove to the main road, and very slowly drove up and down the road, looking and listening for Dad. We were hoping he had crawled back up by the main road so it would be easier for us to load him into the car. We drove about four hundred yards and then decided to turn around and go back toward our house, hoping to spot him on our way back. We pulled onto the main road and started home.

It was then that we noticed the car in front of us had come to a stop in the middle of the road. We slowly pulled up behind the vehicle. A man came back to Mom's car window to tell us that someone was lying in the middle of the road.

Mother told him, "It's my husband." He asked if we needed help to get him in our car, and Mom thanked him for his help. As Mother and I walked by the man's car, I looked in and saw my seventh-grade teacher in the passenger seat. It was her husband who had offered to help. I was so embarrassed. I just knew she would think badly of me from that time forward, but she never mentioned the incident, and I was so glad. We loaded Dad into the car, and he slept there the rest of the night.

SAVED?

One of the most traumatic events of my young life happened while we lived on Bono Hill. One day Dad was drinking and being very abusive to the entire family. There was a knock on the door, and when Mom opened the door, she saw Bill Howard. He had promised to check on us from time to time, and there he was, following up on his promise. It just happened to be when Dad was pulling one of his stunts. Mother invited Bill in. Dad looked like the cat that swallowed the canary—he was speechless, because it was obvious what was going on.

Bill talked to us for a few minutes, and Dad sat down in a leather chair in the corner of the room. Bill turned to Dad and asked if he could pray for him. I don't think Dad quite knew how to react, so he said yes. Pastor Bill knelt in front of the chair where Dad was sitting and started to pray. Almost immediately, Dad screamed out, "Praise God, I'm saved! I'm saved! Praise God!"

Bill Howard arose, patted Dad on the back, turned to Mother, and said, "Kathleen, I will be coming through town after services tonight, and I will check on you guys."

I turned to Tony and whispered, "Dad got saved."

To that Tony replied, "No, he didn't."

"Yes, he did," I insisted. "Didn't you hear what he said?"

Pastor Bill left, and Dad resumed where he had left off just before Bill knocked on the door—namely, screaming and cursing. I looked Dad straight in his face and said, "I thought you got saved." I was devastated to learn what Dad had done. I was the only one in the room who believed he got saved.

Maybe it was wishful thinking on my part, but I just never dreamed that anyone would fake something like that. After this incident, I looked at Dad from a different perspective. I know what the Bible says about honoring your father and mother, but after all the things Dad had done, this was the one that broke my heart.

Mrs. Tompkins had always made the Ten Commandments a focal point. We had discussed this commandment specifically, and it was hard for me to filter something like Dad's behavior through my thirteen-year-old mind. I decided to honor him as my dad but not agree with what he did. A few months later, Dad came home with the news that he had landed a new job. He was going to be the foreman at the McDaniel farm. It was located on Owl City Road near Hoxie, not far from where we'd lived when dad worked on Potters' farm. Dad told us we would have a nice farmhouse in which to live, with running water and an indoor bathroom. We were moving back to the Hoxie school district. I would be back with all the friends I had made the year before. Unlike all of the other moves, I was excited about this one.

5

Life Lessons: Pieces of Trauma and Trust

Chapter 5 is the most difficult for many to read. If you have witnessed or personally experienced verbal and physical abuse, this part of Mike's story may cause you to relive the gamut of emotions. We need people we can trust in our lives, like Bill Howard and Coach Dalson. We also need to realize we have a God we can always trust to help us in life. Consider these examples of God's people helping, even in the most painful parts of Mike's childhood.

Another Adventure

A new adventure can be as simple as a change
of scenery or a change of the heart.

A good attitude can make a new move, new job, or new relationship a positive one. As Mike and his family moved from Dixie to Hoxie, what were some of the changes on which Mike reflected? What drawbacks did they encounter at their new home? How did they turn their move into a positive adventure? Could you have done this? Read Philippians 4:4–8. How do you learn to rejoice in all things? How can praising God in the midst of a problem help you and others?

Stepping Up

A baseball batter can only swing when he steps up to the plate.
The same goes for leadership.

Mike described an encounter with his old Sunday school teacher Bill Howard. Earlier in the book, we discussed the perspective that there are no chance meeting between others and us. With that in mind, what is the difference between a "coincidence" and a "God incident"? The first relies on luck, but the second is led by God. Do you believe that God has a plan for all of our lives? Read Galatians 6:9–10. How did Bill Howard demonstrate what the apostle Paul wrote in this passage? How can you demonstrate these principles to others?

Late Night Show

When a man needs an audience to speak,
he rarely has anything to say.

Domestic violence is a too-well-known experience in some of today's families. This four-part cycle of abuse was labeled and explained by American psychologist Lenore E. Walker. It expresses a simple fourfold pattern, where the cycle starts with tension building that leads to an abusive incident. Then there is a reconciliation, and the cycle ends with calm. Do you see this cycle of behavior in Mike's dad? Is there someone doing this in your life? Read 1 Timothy 5:8. What does this passage express regarding such actions? How can you avoid or break this cycle? If you are experiencing this cycle, whom do you trust to share this with? What are you willing to do to break the cycle and feel safe?

Zigzagging

Alcohol and anger are akin to gas and an open flame
—explosive and destructive.

Proverbs 20:1 states, "Wine is a mocker, strong drink is a brawler, and whoever is led astray by it is not wise." Mike shares some intense experiences in his life that many in today's society will recognize. Have you helped someone in this type of situation? Have you been the victim of events like this? Read Ephesians 5:18 and Luke 21:34. What does God's Word say about the decision to drink in excess? What are you willing to do to safeguard yourself from drinking to excess or any other addiction that can become destructive? Do you know of someone who struggles in an abusive relationship? What resources can you provide for the person to help protect them?

Protect Us

Of all the things to protect in life,
our hearts should be first.

There is a thief among us. He is shrewd, devious, and destructive. According to Jesus, the thief Satan breaks into our hearts (John 10:10). Once inside, Satan can grow bitterness and hatred. Mike told his mom that he would kill his dad if he ever threatened her again. What was his mom's response? How can you protect your heart from becoming bitter? With which person could you identify? Why?

The Coach

*The greatest investment one can make
in life is in another life.*

Read Titus 2:1–5. Was there someone who encouraged you, trained you, and challenged you? What was the result of that person's investment in your life? Mike introduced us to Coach Dalson. What were lessons Mike learned from him? What are some lessons that a coach or mentor has taught you? In Titus 2:1–5, what is the challenge given?

God's Ways

*The very moment we can explain God,
He will cease to be God.*

Mike reflected on the school sports he enjoyed and the memory of a rolling log truck that could have crushed his foot. What was the end result of that reflection? When you look back at what God has done in your life, how can you express your gratitude to Him? Consider Mike's reference to Isaiah 55:8–9. How does this impact your life in the area of both gratitude and trust?

Ray of Sunlight

A light reflected is twice the light.

Have you ever shined a light into a mirror and watched the reflected light beams dance around the room? Matthew 5:14–16 talks about the power of a light. How was Grandpa Simmons's life like a light for Mike? What did Mike consider to be the "greatest gift" one could give to someone? How can you be a light for others in their lives to help them see and receive Jesus as their Savior?

Bono Hill

A city situated on a hill is not the place to stumble.

Have you ever physically tripped and fell? What was the cause, and who was watching? How did you feel? Sometimes people morally fall and negatively impact their lives, reputations, and families. Mike's dad fell morally and caused public humiliation for him and his family. What happened? Psalm 55:22 and 1 Corinthians 10:12–13 provide promises regarding our stability in walking and not stumbling. What are those promises, and how will you apply them in your life?

Saved?

A man that regards not his word will in
the end have no one regard him.

Have you ever given someone your word? Maybe you said, "I promise you!" You say it with enthusiasm, but what happens when it becomes tough to follow through on your word? It may cost you something in the end. What do you do? Mike's dad made a statement that deeply hurt Mike's heart. What was it? What does Matthew 5:37 and James 5:12 tell us about giving our word? Is there someone you have hurt? Do you need to ask forgiveness from that person?

CHAPTER 6

Pieces of Consequences

EXPECTATIONS

We arrived at the McDaniel farm with high expectations since Dad had painted a picture in our minds of a nice house with running water and an indoor bathroom. As we pulled up to the house, I was excited because it was, to my surprise, much nicer than any house in which we had lived for a long time. Dad got out of the U-Haul truck and talked with a man in a red pickup. When he returned, he explained to Mother that people were still occupying the house into which we were supposed to move. Dad said we would have to move into a smaller farmhouse until the foreman's house became available.

With disappointment leading the way, we drove down the lane that led to two more houses—*shacks* would be a more accurate term. After checking out the place, I discovered the inside was worse than I had imagined. These houses really should have been condemned. We unloaded our furniture, and Dad continued to assure Mom that this was a temporary residence.

About six weeks later, Dad came home with the good news: we would be moving into the foreman's house that weekend. Oh, happy day! I could hardly believe my ears; we would finally have a decent house to live in.

The house was all that Dad had described, with hardwood floors, four bedrooms, one bathroom, a living room, and a big eat-in kitchen. To our family, it was a mansion. We got settled, and every night I told God during my nightly prayers, "Thank you for our beautiful house."

I had not attended church for quite a while, but I held strongly to my faith and communicated with God daily through praying and just talking with God about everything going on in my life. Many times I expressed to God that when I grew up, I had no desire to be rich but I asked Him to bless me with a good-paying job, one that would support my family. I always ended my requests by promising to work hard and to always give Him the credit for answering my prayers.

This would be a great time for me to honor God for always providing generously for my family and me. Maybe you would like to join me. To God be the glory!

NO RESCUE

Dad, being the foreman of the farm, decided to put me to work driving a tractor. I had turned fourteen in June, and Dad said, I was old enough to hire in as a full-time farmhand. I was happy about working on the farm, but I really didn't know what I could do. All I had ever done was pick and chop cotton on my grandpa Baird's farm. Tony and I would work on the farm and use the money to buy school clothes. I enjoyed working in the fields. It was hard work, but on Saturdays, Uncle Carl, the uncle who helped our family when we lived in Weiner, would come and work with us until noon. I loved Uncle Carl, and working with him was fun because he would joke with us boys and make the workday seem like a play day.

The farm where we now lived was a different kind of farm. It was more of a corporate farm where all the grounds were planted in soy beans and rice—big money crops. Along with a farm like this came the need for big, expensive equipment and for ground wells to water the crops. In those days, most small farmers like Grandpa couldn't afford to install in-ground wells to water and maintain these types of crops.

The much-anticipated morning came, and Dad walked me to where the farmhands were preparing their tractors for another day. Dad introduced me to some of the other men and then walked me to what he called a 930 Case tractor. In my mind, it was huge, but compared to some of the other equipment, not so much. Dad said, "This is the tractor you will be driving today, and you will be pulling a disk behind you."

"Dad," I said, "I don't know how to drive this tractor."

"Just do what I say, and everything will be okay," he told me.

There was a lot of laughing, cursing, and storytelling going on by the other men, and I felt like a duck out of my pond. I just listened and observed what was going on around me, kept my mouth shut, and tried to stay out of everyone's way. Dad drove the tractor with me to the field where I would be working and gave me specific instructions. He said to leave the disk in the ground, and when I wanted to stop, I was to hit the clutch, and the weight and pull of the disk in the ground would stop me. I drove all morning with no problems. We ate lunch in the field, and then I was back on the tractor until around six o'clock when we ended our workday. I was feeling good that I'd not experienced any problems at all. I raised the disk out of the ground like Dad had instructed me to do. I pointed my tractor in the direction of the equipment shed and headed in behind the other tractors.

The day was pretty much over, and I felt good about myself. As we came into the place where the tractors were stored, I saw everyone parking the tractors in a lean-to—a stall with a slanted roof in the back that protected the tractors from the weather. I followed in line as each one pulled slowly in to his lean-to. As I pulled in, I hit my clutch because that was what I had been doing all day. However, my disk was not in the ground, so I didn't stop. My tractor ran right through the lean-to and came out on the other side. I stopped, but the stall was plowed through, and the smokestack on the tractor was ripped off. I immediately realized what I had done wrong, but it was too late. Dad was at my side, and he wasn't happy with me.

Dad called me many names that day, and as I tried to explain I realized I was making matters worse. The best thing was to just be quiet. I was very sorry I had made that mistake, but mostly I was sorry I had embarrassed Dad in front of the other farmhands. It is not a good feeling for a young boy to know his dad is ashamed of him. I thought of that incident many times throughout my young adult life. I still remember the laughter of the other farmhands and how great it would have been if Dad had come to my rescue, but that's not how it worked out for me that day.

I wish I could say just once that Dad watched out for me and stood by my side. It would be great to write this story and make Dad my hero, but I can't do that. I have learned that people will often disappoint us, but God will never let us down. I am so grateful we have a loving heavenly Father who does not treat His children with disrespect, even when we mess up.

SELF-PRESERVATION

When I went home that afternoon, Mother asked me what was wrong, and I told her what had happened. Dad came in shortly after me. He was still very upset and continued to call me names. Mother told him to stop. One thing led to another, and it ended in a big fight, with Dad leaving in the company truck.

We ate supper late that night, and then Mother told us to get ready for bed. When we went to bed around nine o'clock, Dad had not yet returned home. I was glad to call it a day. I wanted to go to bed and forget about what had happened. Unfortunately, that would not be the case. Around one o'clock in the morning, I awoke to the sound of screaming and hollering. I lay in my bed, hoping it would stop, but it didn't. Tony and I shared a bedroom, and suddenly the door to our room opened. Dad shouted at us to get out of bed. He took us into the kitchen, where he had told Mother to cook supper again. He said he wanted the entire family to be seated at the table to eat together. At Dad's demand, Mom fried chicken and made mashed potatoes with gravy. There we were at 1:30 in the morning, seated at the table, with Dad telling us to eat.

As we ate, Dad picked at Mother. It was obvious he was trying to start an argument. Mom was very quiet, trying to appease him, but when Mother would not argue with him, he became enraged. As we all sat at the table, Dad put his arms under the edge of the table and flipped it over, causing food and dishes to fly all over the kitchen.

Cindy was seated next to Dad, and as he flipped the table, he knocked over the chair where she was sitting. A shard from one of the broken dishes hit her face, cutting her lip very deeply—blood poured from the wound. Mother grabbed a dish towel and pressed it against the cut. Within minutes, the towel was soaked with Cindy's blood. Mother told Dad we needed to take her to the hospital, but Dad refused, insisting everything would be okay. Dad sobered up quickly. He held Cindy in his arms and wouldn't let Mother look at the wound.

We didn't take Cindy to the hospital, and she still carries the scar on her lip from that night's tragedy. Thinking back, I am certain Dad believed he would be arrested if Mother reported what had happened. It is hard to imagine a dad allowing his child to go without medical attention to protect himself. It was always my fear that Dad would accidently hurt one of us kids or Mother during one of his tirades. This time, it just happened to be our sister, Cindy. I am thankful no one was ever killed.

LIFE OR LOSS

A few weeks later Mother became sick and went to the doctor. When she came home, she told us we were going to have a new baby brother or sister. That would make number five. You might be wondering why or how this could happen. A new baby was probably the last thing our family needed. Remember we didn't have medical insurance, we never went to the doctor, and I am certain Mom wasn't using contraception.

I am thankful this took place in 1965, when abortion was still against the law in Arkansas. If it had been 2016, Mother could have been encouraged to have an abortion. I don't know what Mom would have done if it had been legal to abort a child. I don't think she would have considered it, because sanctity of life was always important to Mother.

A few months later, my baby sister Charlotte Ann was born. She has grown up to be a kind and loving person. She became a schoolteacher in the Walnut Ridge, Arkansas, public school system. She was one of four finalists for Teacher of the Year for the state of Arkansas in 2000. More recently, she became a professor and the edTAP teacher performance assessment coordinator at Williams Baptist College in Walnut Ridge (she is Charlotte Wheeless, MEd, NBCT [national board certified teacher] Department of Education and a third-year doctoral student in 2016, pursuing an educational degree in organizational leadership, with an emphasis in higher education.

Charlotte is a blessing to me, our family, and countless other lives. She loves the Lord and loves to share her faith and teaching knowledge with the young adult students at the college. Her students consider themselves lucky to attend her classes, and she considers each of her students a precious gift from God. What a travesty if she had been aborted and what a loss to the world. I can't help but think of the millions of beautiful lives that have been aborted and the contributions their lives could have made to our society.

A BREAK OF A LIFETIME

One day there was a knock on our door. Cindy ran to tell Mother someone was on our porch—we didn't receive company very often. Mom answered the door. It was a well-dressed man who introduced himself as Pastor Andy, the new pastor at the Church of the Nazarene. He informed us he had taken Bill Howard's place at the church and asked if he could come in and visit. By this time we kids had gathered in the living room; we wanted to hear what he had to say.

We had one chair in the corner of the room, out of the way. We kept the old chair because we didn't have enough furniture, and the chair helped to fill the big living room. One of the legs on the chair was loose. If we sat still in the chair, everything would be okay, but if we moved or wiggled around, the leg would come loose, and we would come tumbling down.

I watched the pastor eye that chair and thought perhaps Mom would lead him to another place to sit, but no such luck. He sat in the broken chair. We all kept our mouths shut, hoping for the best. I looked at Tony; he had a half smile on his face because we both knew what was about to happen. Although I didn't want the pastor to fall, I didn't know how to prevent it from happening, so Tony and I just sat still and watched the show. The pastor wiggled as he talked, the leg came loose from the chair, and to the floor he fell. I must admit it was quite funny. As the pastor was saying how sorry he was for breaking our chair, I heard the kitchen door open. It was Dad.

Mother introduced him to the pastor. Much to my surprise, they hit it off and had a great conversation. It turned out the pastor was an electrician. He said he currently was working in a government missile silo, and he mentioned to Dad how much they needed qualified people to work there. This gave Dad an opportunity to talk about his experience and the different licenses he had acquired.

"Would you be interested in pursuing a job?" the pastor asked.

Dad immediately responded, "What do I need to do?"

"You'll need to join the electrical workers union."

"That's not a problem," Dad said.

"You'll also need to take a written test," Pastor Andy said, "but I can help with some material for you to study."

A few weeks later Dad went with Pastor Andy to take the required test. Dad was an intelligent man, and he passed the test with a high score. He joined the union with the help and recommendation of the pastor and was immediately hired at the missile silo.

Dad came home and gave his notice at the McDaniel farm, and a few weeks later he went to work at his new job. Dad's farming days were over. It was the break of a lifetime and a job of which he had dreamed. Ironically, Dad had gotten the job with, of all things, the help of a pastor. I thought surely this was "a God thing." What were the chances of something like that just happening in a man's life?

DIFFERENT DIRECTIONS

The entire family was excited, but Dad was exuberant. He couldn't stop talking about what had happened. I wondered if he ever considered God's roll in this obvious blessing, but his conversation was primarily about himself. Dad always loved to brag about how talented he was. Many times he said, "If they would have asked me, I could have told them what to do and saved them a lot of time."

I know God had a hand in making all that happen. The thing is, His ways and thoughts are higher than ours, and His plan does not always coincide with ours. Sometimes God does something so dramatic—sometimes even catastrophic—in our lives, only to move us in a different direction, one in which the pieces of our life puzzles never would have materialized without the right set of circumstances.

We moved quickly from the farm to Walnut Ridge. We lived there a few months and then moved into a little house back in Hoxie, at the south end of town. This was the time when our sister, Charlotte Ann, was born. Dad's new job took him away from home for a week at a time. At first, he would come home every weekend. After a while he would be gone for two weeks at a time. I knew Mother was concerned about Dad's being away so much and not coming home over the weekend. When he did come home, he seemed distant and removed from the life of our family.

One Saturday afternoon Dad pulled up to our house in a new sports car. He came inside and talked privately with Mother in the kitchen. Then they gathered us kids together in the living room, and Mom said Dad had something he wanted to say. Dad told us about a wonderful family he had met. He said the children called him Daddy, and he had met a wonderful woman with whom he had fallen in love. He finished by telling us, "I'll be living with them from now on."

No one said a word; we all looked at Mother to see her response. Mother never revealed her true feelings; she simply said, "I wanted you to hear this from your dad."

As Dad drove away, his words were still ringing in my ears. I wondered how Mother felt, so that night I asked her, "What are we going to do?"

Her reply was an honest one: "I really don't know."

A CHANGE FOR THE BETTER

I can't even imagine the pressure Mother must have felt with five children (one in a crib), no job (she hadn't worked in years), no car, and very little money because we always lived from paycheck to paycheck. This was not the first time Dad had put a heavy burden on Mother's shoulders, leaving her to deal with circumstances that would have been unbearable for anyone. I believe Mother did a lot of praying during this time, asking God for guidance. How do I know she turned to the Lord? Simply, I know my mother, and I know how she thought.

That night as I lay in bed, I thought back to a question I had asked God on that cold and snowy gravel road, where

I'd fallen from my bike. In my desperation I'd asked God why we had to live like this. Although I again asked God the same question, I didn't realize that God was in the process of creating pieces of our life puzzle that would change our lives for the better. We just needed time to place those pieces in our puzzle where they belonged.

I thank God that my mother was a strong-willed woman. She bought a paper the next morning and began looking for a job. Tony, my older brother, saw a job listed for the local radio station, KRLW, in Walnut Ridge. They needed someone to read the news from the AP wire. Tony told Mother he was going to apply for the job. Although Tony was not quite sixteen years old, the chances of a teenager getting that job seemed slim—or so we thought.

It's true that God can do anything He pleases and can make things happen in any way He chooses. He is always so far ahead of us. I love knowing and understanding how our God works. It makes this Baptist boy want to have a Pentecostal moment.

As I mentioned earlier, Tony would read any book or magazine he could get his hands on. None of us knew, but God had started preparing him years earlier for such a time as this. He applied for the job and later told us that after he read for them, they told him to come back to read the next day—only this time he would read on the air.

The next day at 5:00 p.m., our family gathered around the radio tuned to KRLW. Tony read the news so beautifully in his crystal-clear baritone voice; he didn't make one mistake. God had blessed Tony with his beautiful voice and with the talent to land that job. Soon, Tony had his own show and became well known around town.

Tony was hired at the salary of one hundred dollars per week, and he bought a car for three hundred dollars. Mother landed a job with a government agency called BRAD (Black River Area Development). She started as a teacher's aide. This job's intent was to provide someone from a low-income family with a place for her children to stay while she worked. That meant Mother could take Charlotte to work with her. God had provided a way for our family. Tony got the first job and really helped our family, buying groceries and helping Mother in many ways. Tony and Mother arranged a way for them both to use Tony's car for transportation. Soon, Mother bought a used car for herself and solved the transportation problem.

I always appreciated what Tony and Mother accomplished. God had blessed them both with talents, and they used them to take care of our family in our time of need. The things God did for our family back then seem almost unbelievable now, but God is an amazing God and is worthy to be praised!

6

Life Lessons: Pieces of Consequences

In chapter 6, Mike described a number of ups and downs in his family life. Regardless of the choices one makes, there always are consequences. For the most part, we consider the word *consequence* as having a negative meaning, yet when we do the right thing, we experience good consequences. As you read the following, determine where you stand.

Expectations

Successful expectation management is experienced
by having harmony in the requests given and
the acceptance of the answer provided.

Have you ever heard the phrase, "One step forward and two steps back"? In Mike's case, it was two houses back. When you pray and ask God for a blessing, how long are you willing to wait? What do you do in the meantime while God is preparing to answer your request with His best? Isaiah 40:28–31 provides a wonderful principle about waiting on the Lord. Write down blessings that have come to you while waiting for God.

No Rescue

It is a sad moment in life when we find out that
our security rope, used to prevent a fall, was
never tied to anything that would help.

Are you confident when you try something new? Clear instructions are a crucial factor for good results. As Mike found out while driving the tractor, doing what seemed right could lead to disastrous results. When in your life did you choose to take a shortcut, and what were the results? How did others treat you afterward? Do you think that God would ever treat you as Mike's dad treated him? Read Psalm 91 for the answer, and write down how God would be a sure rescue for you in your need.

Self-Preservation

When God commanded you to guard your heart,
it was so that you would also learn how to guard
the hearts of others.

What does it mean to be other-focused? Read Ephesians 4:1–3. What happens when you think only about yourself? What negative consequences have resulted from self-preserving actions and attitudes? Ephesians 4:12–16 provides the necessary steps toward becoming other-focused. Which one could you commit to do this week?

Life or Loss

A triumphant start of life comes when we choose
to save and love life and, in the end,
give him or her a name.

As a parent, are you able to provide for your kids? Can God provide for you? A choice that Christians must make is to trust God. When we trust, we learn that God is faithful and that blessings can come from hard times. All of Charlotte's adult accomplishments came from her mom's decision to trust God to take care of the needs of her family. In Matthew 6:26–34, Jesus provided a picture of God's provisions. What were they, and how can you use them to understand? How can you help others to understand?

Break of a Lifetime

The difference between a handout and a hand is what
you are willing to do with it once you receive it.

In this section, Mike described two breaks. The first was an old chair, and the second was his dad's silence toward preachers. What was the catalyst that created a great conversation between the Nazarene pastor and Mike's dad? Read 1 Peter 1:1–5. When we talk with others, our faith should be evident in the conversation. Are you able to have that type of conversation? If so, how do you make sure that Christ is shared when you talk with others?

Different Direction

The devastating detours in our lives can lead to either
a dead end in our travels or a new direction in our
journey. The choice will depend on what map you use.

Mike and his family were blessed financially, and his dad
finally had a dream job, but his dad came home less often
and was emotionally distant when he was at home. Then
Mike's world came apart again. What words could describe
Mike's emotions on hearing his dad's news? Why do you
think Mike's mom had his dad tell the family about his new
direction? What does it mean to take personal responsibility
for your decisions? First Corinthians 10:1–13 holds a sobering
lesson on personal accountability before God. What are those
lessons? What is God's promise when we are tempted to
choose evil? How can you encourage someone to not make
the same mistake that the Israelites made?

A Change for the Better

Change for the sake of change creates frustration.
Change that sparks needed change creates a future.

Have you ever read epitaphs on tombstones? Although
headstones may be different in appearance, they have a couple
of items in common: a date of birth and a date of death. In
between these two dates is a dash. This small etching on the
stone represents what we have done between those two dates.
In this chapter, Mike reminded us that we can look at tragedy

as the end of all good things, or we can trust God to lead us through to a brighter future. In Joel 2:1–32, God promised to redeem, restore, and repair the nation of Israel. He can do the same for you! How might this look in your life?

CHAPTER 7

Pieces of Maturity

PAYING OUR WAY

With Dad gone, life became somewhat normal around our house. Mother got a job, but as you might imagine, the pay as a teacher's aide was not much. It was enough, however, if we watched our pennies. Mother was an ambitious woman. She had no intention of staying in one position very long and soon was moved to a teaching position.

We were all proud of Tony and would listen to his radio show when at all possible. He was very good as a radio announcer and became quite popular with adults as well as teenagers. They would call in and request songs for their friends, and Tony gained positive notoriety around our small town.

I was fourteen years old and needed a steady job. I went around the town, asking about employment, but sixteen was the age required for businesses to legally hire someone, and I was about eighteen months shy of that. I walked the streets of Hoxie and Walnut Ridge, and if I saw people working in their yards or on small projects, I would stop to ask if they needed help. I landed several jobs using that tactic. When they asked what I would charge for my work, I would say, "Just pay me what you think I'm worth." I was accustomed to working hard day labor on the farm and was not afraid of work. I knew if they were fair-minded people, they would pay me accordingly.

I finally got a job as a carhop at the Walnut Ridge Polar Freeze, a popular local teenager hamburger-and-shake hangout. I was paid thirty cents per hour plus tips. I would go to work at four o'clock in the afternoon and work until closing, which was any time from midnight to 1:30 a.m. I was glad to get that job and worked three to five nights every week. It was a fast-paced job. Sometimes on Friday and Saturday nights, fifteen to twenty cars were on the lot at the same time. I made enough money to buy my school clothes, pay for school lunches, and supply myself with spending money. By our working, Tony and I took a great burden off Mother; we were essentially paying our own ways. The owner of the Polar Freeze, Mr. Jack Allison, would bring me home after closing, as he did for all the teenagers who worked for him. Jack watched out for us kids, and we all respected him greatly.

The old Polar Freeze building has been torn down, but I stop by the new building when I am in town. I always look for Jack, just to say hello and of course to grab a barbecue or Big Boy sandwich, for which he is famous.

When Jack brought me home from work, no matter what time it was, Mother and I would count my tip change, put it in a bowl, and place it on the table. I used that money as I needed it, and Mother knew she could take change to pay for school lunches for my brother and sister. School lunches cost twenty cents and were well worth the money. I also worked in the school cafeteria whenever they needed me. The mother of one of my school friends, Richard Tinker, was the manager. He and I both enjoyed working with the cafeteria ladies, and the fringe benefits included free lunches and as many refills on food as we could eat. It was great, certainly not what I would call hard work, and I was thankful for the opportunity.

AWKWARD REUNION

Our family returned to the Church of the Nazarene. We felt thankful that God was providing for our family. One Sunday afternoon, we had just arrived home from church when there was a knock on the door. It was Dad, only this time he was not driving that new sports car. He told Mother that they needed to talk. Mom and Dad went into the kitchen, and when they came out Dad visited with us. He didn't stay long because no one was very talkative—the last time we'd seen him, he told us about his new "family." Those words were still ringing in our ears, so it didn't make for a cozy reunion.

After he was gone, Mother gathered us at the kitchen table and explained what was going on. Mother said, "Your dad wants to come back and live with us. He feels he made a mistake by leaving and wants to start over." Mom told us to take our time to think about the situation and then to let her know our thoughts.

I followed Mother to her bedroom and asked if I could talk to her.

"You need to take some time and think about this issue before we discuss it further," she said.

"Mom, I don't have to think about this," I said. "I already know how I feel, and my vote is that there's no way we should let him come back. For the first time since we have lived in the Blue House we have peace in our home. We no longer have to sit up at night, waiting for Dad to come home drunk, wondering what he would do or who he would beat up."

"If we tell him no," Mom told me, "we will have to move from here because we can't afford the rent."

"Then let's move," I said. "If he came back, we'd be moving anyway because he would either lose his job or get fired—and who knows where we'd end up." I felt like God had provided an opportunity so we would never have to live like that again. I said, "Mom, we can make it without him and will have a much happier life, so please don't let him come back."

STANDING YOUR GROUND

I talked with Tony later and asked him if he had talked to Mother.

He nodded. "I told Mom I will move out of the house if Dad comes back." Tony had a job and had no intention of ever living in the same house with Dad again.

A few days later Dad returned to our house. I saw his clothes hanging in the backseat of his car, and I thought, *He thinks he's here to stay.* Tony was at work, and I was glad for him because he didn't have to go through the ordeal that I knew was coming. When Dad entered the house, Mother explained that she had made the decision that he could not come back.

Dad was not happy with her answer. "I have no place to go," he informed her. "Therefore, I'm moving back into the house." Dad's voice had taken on a more demanding tone; whereas before he had asked, now he was telling Mother he was back.

I was proud of Mom. She never showed any sign of giving in, nor did she give any indication that she might change her mind. Mom looked straight in his face and said, "Freddy, if I have to call the police on you, I will, but you are not moving your clothes back into our house."

I was lurking in the shadows of the hallway because Mom had sent me out of the room. I thought I should stay close in case she needed me, but she didn't need me or anyone else. At last she'd stood up to him. He left.

THE PRESENT

Mother began the search for another rental house, one we could afford. I was proud that when we moved, we did not owe any money for past rent. Mother did this the right way, and I was proud of her. We moved to another house in Hoxie not far from school, close enough for us to walk. It was not a pretty house—the outside needing painting badly—but Mom could afford the rent at forty-five dollars per month.

We didn't hear from Dad for several months, and then one day the telephone rang, and it was him. He wanted to come by with some Christmas presents, but he didn't know where we were living. At first Mother was hesitant to give him our address, but it was only a few weeks until Christmas, and he convinced her he just wanted to see his kids. Dad came by and brought with him a bag of Christmas presents wrapped in nice holiday paper. He distributed the presents and then retreated to the bathroom. He'd given me some cologne. I always loved cologne; back then, English Leather, High Karate, or Brut were the popular men's colognes. I don't remember what Dad bought me, but I liked anything that smelled good.

I noticed another present in Dad's bag. I looked at the tag; it read "Mother." I was happy that Dad remembered to buy Mother a present. In my mind, she deserved a present more than any of us. Mother was sitting on the couch, and I said to her, "Mom, there is a present for you."

"Really?" she said. I handed the gift to her, and she unwrapped it. It was a lady's powder and cologne set. When Dad came back into the living room, Mom said, "Freddy, thank you for the present. You didn't have to buy me anything."

"What are you talking about?" he asked. Mom held up the powder set, and Dad said, "That's not yours. That's for my mother, not you."

The room became totally silent—we were barely breathing, let alone talking.

"I am so sorry," Mother said, as her face turned four shades of red. "I can rewrap it for you."

Words cannot express the way I felt, and it was partly my fault since I'd handed the present to Mother. I knew she was not just embarrassed but also deeply hurt, and so was I. It still hurts me today. There are some things I will never forget.

Dad said, "Just keep it. I'll get my mother something else."

"Absolutely not!" Mother responded.

I handed Dad my cologne and said, "Here, you can give this to someone else. I don't want it." He tried to insist that I keep it, but I said, "You should not have brought a present into this house with 'Mother' written on it. You should have kept presents for other people in your car."

All he would have had to do was keep his mouth shut. No one would have known, and we would have given him credit for doing something decent for Mother. I could not imagine how anyone could be so insensitive and cruel to a person to whom he had been married for over twenty years and with whom he had five children.

There's an old saying, "Sticks and stones may break my bones, but words can never hurt me." That's not in the Bible, and it's a lie. Negative words *do* hurt people, and they can never be taken back, once spoken. We should be more sensitive concerning what we say to someone or about someone. People can forgive us for what we say, but they may find it difficult to forget.

DUPLEX

We didn't know at the time, but when Mother was looking for a new house we could afford, she applied for a duplex that was considered government housing. This duplex was fairly new, and the rent was supported by the Department of Housing and Urban Development, better known as HUD. The duplexes were built for people with limited income, and we certainly fit into that category. A letter came stating that we had been accepted; a duplex was available if we were still interested.

This was almost too good to be true. In a very short span of time, God had supplied Mother, Tony, and me with jobs; Mother had bought a car; and now a beautiful new duplex was made available to our family. The pieces of our life puzzle were falling into place. It was apparent that God was doing some wonderful things in our lives. We moved into the duplex and lived there until I graduated from high school. The rent was $37.50 per month, subsidized by HUD. I was so proud to call it home. It was the nicest house we had ever had. Tony got married before we moved, but Mom essentially raised the rest of us kids in that government duplex.

Several years passed, and I had long since moved away from home. One day Mother told me she was buying a prefabricated house for $14,500.

"Why would you want to move?" I asked.

"When the duplex became available, our family really needed a nice place to live," she said. "Now I can afford to buy this little house and I feel it's only right to free up the duplex so another family in need will have a nice place to raise their children."

I just hugged her and said, "Mom, you are an amazing woman, and I love you."

MOUSE OR MAN

My mother worked a full-time job while she went to college at night. After several years, she obtained her degree. Mother raised all five of us children; she cooked, cleaned, and kept us all straight. Most of all, I give her credit for keeping us all together through some tough times. Often when I was in high school, I would come home from a date, and Mom would get up from bed to be with me. She would fry me a hamburger, sit at the kitchen table with me, and say, "Tell me all about your date." It would be past midnight, and she had to be up by five in the morning, but she took time to be with me. I would tell her everything, and we would laugh and enjoy each other's company. She really was an amazing woman and a great mother. I miss her very much.

Mom knew her children, and she knew I had gone through a period of having negative feeling about myself. I felt as though I had nothing to contribute to conversations, nothing that anyone would be interested in hearing. She knew I was still suffering as a teenager from those feelings of being inferior. Because of my negative feelings about myself, I was very quiet around people, particularly in crowds. I mentioned earlier that my family had nicknamed me Mouse, which I hated.

One night Mom and I were talking. "I want to tell you a story," she said. "There were two young men, both smart and hardworking, but one was outgoing and the other was withdrawn and wouldn't talk to people. They grew up, got married, and had families of their own. The one who was outgoing got a great job. He worked very hard and provided well for his family. The other young man, who was just as smart and hardworking, never provided well for his family. He was not able to make very many friends, and he had a hard time communicating with people." Mom then asked, "Which of the young men do you want to be?"

"The good provider," I replied.

"Then you need to come out of your shell and start talking with people, or you may never be successful in life, although you have the ability to be and do anything you want to do."

I knew Mom was right. I went to bed that night asking God to help me with my negative feelings about myself. I promised God and myself that I was going to make a change and start talking to people. It took a while, but when I overcame my shyness, a new world was revealed to me. I am so appreciative that Mother took the time to lovingly help me with my problem. With God's help, we overcame that struggle. Again I declare, she was an amazing mother.

HIGH-TOPS

I was sixteen years old and driving the bus for the Church of the Nazarene. I enjoyed driving the bus. It was actually a Volkswagen van, and sometimes I would make two trips around town to get everyone picked up. I knew all the folks by name, both young and old. It was a blessing for me to do something for the Lord. Just because I was going to church, however, doesn't mean I would not make mistakes, and I made my share.

I left my job at the Polar Freeze when I turned sixteen and started working at Rorex AG supermarket. The minimum wage was $1.65 per hour, but many of us high school boys were working there, so our hours were limited. I was playing basketball for Hoxie High School, the home of the Mustangs. I loved playing ball and actually loved the practices as much as the games. I loved the smell of the locker room, if that tells you anything. I would have rather played a game of ball than eat, and that sums it up, especially coming from a teenage boy.

I had saved my money for a long time and bought a pair of high-top All-Star Converse tennis shoes. In the year 1967, a pair of these shoes was vastly important to a guy's overall image and appearance on the court. They were like gold to me.

One day I went to practice and noticed the combination lock on my locker was broken. I looked inside—and my shoes were missing. I couldn't believe someone had taken my beautiful high-top All-Star Converse shoes. I reported what had happened to the coach, but I could tell it wasn't as important to him as it was devastating to me.

"Do you have another pair?" he asked.

"No, I have an old pair of plain tennis shoes but not like the ones missing."

"Wear what you have until you can buy another pair." He acted like I could just go to the store and replace them. He obviously didn't understand how long I had saved to buy those shoes. I couldn't just "buy another pair." I missed practice that day, went home, and found my old low-top shoes. I cleaned them up as best I could. I still couldn't believe someone had done this to me.

JUSTIFYING

About two weeks later, we were playing an away game, and to my surprise, I saw a pair of high-top All-Star Converse shoes in an unlocked locker. They were size 10, my size. I slipped my old shoes off and laced the newly found Converse shoes on my feet. I played in them that night, and when we left the gym, I brought the shoes home with me.

A few days later, I went to the gym for our regular practice, but the coach caught me as I arrived and asked to see me in his office. As I walked in, I saw the shoes I'd taken sitting on his desk.

"Do you recognize these shoes?" he asked.

I replied, "Yes, they are just like the ones that were stolen from me several weeks ago."

"Did you steal these shoes?" he asked.

"No," I said. "I replaced the ones that were stolen from me."

"Do you remember the day you found your locker empty?" he asked. "Do you recall how you felt?"

I said, "I remember."

"What you did was exactly what you hated."

I knew he was right. I was wrong, and the coach was right. It only took his speaking the truth to make me realize what I had done.

He was silent for what seemed a long time. I didn't say anything either. Finally, the coach broke the silence by saying, "I think we need to return these shoes, don't you?"

I managed to say yes. My head hung low, and I felt a sick feeling in the pit of my soul that I will never forget.

The coach said, "I have thought about how to handle this and have decided you will be off the team for the rest of the year."

"Okay," I replied. The coach took away the one thing I dearly loved, but knowing I deserved the punishment hurt worse than losing the right to play ball. This piece to my life puzzle provided a lesson I have never forgotten.

As I left the office, I turned to the coach and said, "Would you tell them I'm sorry for what I did?" I really meant it. In life, certain situations happen, things we remember all our lives. Sometimes these situations are devastating at the time, but serve us later in life as a guide to the right way of thinking. I learned that day about consequences surrounding my actions, even when I'm sorry.

Can you imagine standing before our righteous God, trying to explain to Him that your actions in life were warranted? You mistreated someone because that person mistreated you. Can you imagine trying to convince God that you deserve heaven because of all of the good deeds you have done?

SHOES AND SOULS

I lost the right to play ball, but I recouped from that loss and moved forward with my life after learning a valuable lesson. The truth: if we never ask Jesus to forgive our sins and never ask Him to be our Savior, we will lose everything. We will have no hope of regrouping and making changes. It will all be over. Can you imagine looking down at your life puzzle and seeing the main piece, Jesus, missing? Talk about a sick feeling in the depth of our souls. To be separated from God and hopelessly lost forever is unfathomable.

I am reminded of the question Jesus asked: "For what shall it profit a man, if he shall gain the whole world, and lose his own soul?" (Mark 8:36 KJV). If you have never asked Jesus to save you, I am compelled to include this invitation just for you. If God is speaking to your heart, pray this prayer while there is still time. Add this piece to your life puzzle:

> Father, I confess to you that I am a sinner. I believe that the Lord Jesus Christ died for my sins on the cross and was raised for my justification, and I do now receive and confess Him as my personal Savior.

Romans 10:9 states, "That if thou shalt confess with thy mouth the Lord Jesus, and shalt believe in thine heart that God hath raised him from the dead, thou shalt be saved."

DRAMA CLASS

I had overcome my shyness for the most part, and I decided to take a class in speech and drama that was offered during my junior and senior years of high school. I wanted to take the class because Hoxie High had recruited a new teacher, Mrs. Vaughn. Rumor had it she had volunteered to teach the class and was doing it without getting a salary. I can't confirm that rumor, but I can tell you she was a very classy lady. She had an air of sophistication about her like no other teacher at Hoxie High School.

It also was rumored that she was an actress and had played character roles on the television series *Gunsmoke* with actor James Arness. I studied under her direction for two years. Speech and drama soon became my favorite class, and performing the skits did wonders for my self-esteem. Sometimes Mrs. Vaughn would ask me to stay late to do a skit for the following class. I did whatever she asked of me because I knew she was sincere, and she made me feel special.

Mrs. Vaughn will never know what her kindness and special attention did for me throughout my life. I needed encouragement and confidence, and she gave it to me. Thank God for great teachers!

THE MEDAL

Near the end of my senior year, I joined the National Guard. I would have to miss my senior graduation by a few days to obtain the MOS [military occupational specialty] I wanted. One afternoon Mrs. Vaughn asked to see me after class. I couldn't imagine what she wanted. She said, "I heard you will not be at your graduation. Is that true?"

"Yes, it is," I said, and I explained my situation.

"My plan was to award you the speech medal." It was an award given every year to a gifted junior or senior. "You earned the medal, but since you won't be at graduation, I will announce your name as the winner of this year's medal during the next school assembly."

"I can't believe it," I said.

Then she said something to me that meant more than any medal I could ever receive: "Mike, I don't have children, but if I did, I would love to have a son just like you."

I have never forgotten her words. She may not have fully realized at the time what her words meant to me, but it was one of the greatest gifts anyone has ever given me—a gift of sentiment and words that I could never repay.

The school assembly was called, and the announcement

was made that I had won the speech medal that year. A classmate named Becky turned to me and said, "When did you get smart?" I replied, "When Mrs. Vaughn came to town."

Mother went to my graduation in my absence and received my diploma and the speech medal, presented by Mrs. Vaughn. To Mother, it was a big deal; she talked about that incident for years. I have only looked at the medal a couple of times throughout my entire life. Today, I don't even know where it is. It wasn't the tangible medal that I cherished; it was Mrs. Vaughn's words that made all the difference in my world. Her words can never be lost or stolen from my memory. I still recall with appreciation this learned teacher who, through her kindness and love of her students, changed my perspective on life.

Was this merely a coincidence? No. I believe God knows what you and I need in our lives. People, places, and things are placed before us with His perfect timing in order to accomplish His perfect will. God knew what I needed, and He used a well-respected schoolteacher to encourage me.

He also knows all about your life, and He is no respecter of persons. What He will do for one, He will do for all.

7

Life Lessons: Pieces of Maturity

In this chapter, Mike and his brother took the needed steps to mature into responsible young men. Mike also described other situations where taking responsibility was not high on his agenda. The best picture of maturity is not found in the number of years lived but in how one lives those years.

Paying Our Way

A joy shared is a double joy.
A burden shared is only half a burden.

What is the difference between hard work and working hard? The first describes the physical difficulty of a task. The second is a commitment to get something done. The first depends on our skill and knowledge. The second depends on our positive attitude, character, and integrity. Mike shared how he and Tony worked hard to share the burden of family financial responsibility. What did that demonstrate about their characters? Remember that a burden is lighter when shared. Read Galatians 6:2. Have you helped "share the load" with someone? If so, why did you do it? What did you do?

Awkward Reunion

An awkward moment is when a lie knocks on
the door of your heart, and truth answers it.

Do you know the expression, "the elephant in the room"? Mike described such an experience with his dad. Mike made a strong plea for his mom not to take his dad back into the home. Why? Have you experienced this type of encounter? How did you handle it? Take a moment to read James 1:2–5. How do you consider requests from others, especially from children, when considering sensitive issues?

Standing Your Ground

The house of the heart has many rooms,
but the most important part is the lock on the front door.

What is God's purpose of accountability and responsibility? Mike's mom did not back down when she encountered the anger of her husband. What happened? How did she hold Mike's dad accountable for his actions? Why do you think Mike's dad tried to intimidate her? Proverbs 29:22–23 and Proverbs 19:19 provide a perspective on that answer. In what ways could you hold others accountable for their actions?

The Wrong Present

A pretty package does not a present make.

Mike described a sad situation in which each of the kids received a present from his father, but his mom did not. Although she opened a gift with "Mother" written on it, it was not her gift. How did you feel when you read that? Why is the saying "sticks and stones …" a lie? How did Mike react?

What would you have done? James 3:1–12 reminds us of how our words and actions can hurt others. Why is that important to remember?

Duplex

How do you make a single blessing into a double blessing? You are willing to share the first blessing with someone else.

Take a moment to read Proverbs 11:25. Mike described some wonderful blessings that the family received. Read back through that section of this chapter and write them down. Take the time to write down some of the blessings you have encountered this week. Why was Mike's mom willing to move out of the duplex and into another house when she did not have to move? Would you have been willing to do the same? As you consider Proverbs 11:25, write down your thoughts on how you can turn a single blessing into a double blessing.

Man or Mouse

The first place that a man must stand to be recognized is within the hallways of his own heart.

Mike's mom talked with Mike about the type of man he was and the type of man he wanted to be. When was the last time you had to "speak the truth in love" (Ephesians 4:15) to someone? Has someone ever needed to speak this way to you? What does it take for a person to be ready to hear the truth?

Read 2 Samuel 12. The prophet Nathan spoke truth to King David. How can a story be helpful in talking with someone about a needed change in his or her life?

High-Tops

True satisfaction from a purchased item lies not in the object but in the knowledge that you worked hard to get it.

Have you ever worked so you could buy something special? What was it? Mike bought a special pair of shoes with his hard-earned money. Those shoes not only filled a need on the basketball courts, but they were also a fashion statement. Mike's shoes were stolen. If something was ever stolen from you, how did you feel? Read Matthew 6:19–21. What can we keep safe from the thieves of this world?

Away Game

The difference between justified and justifying is the sleep you get at night.

During the away game, Mike found a pair of high-tops that were just his size. What did he do? Why? What happens when we try to justify our actions? The great preacher Matthew Henry reflected on an incident in which he was robbed and his wallet was taken. Henry said, "I am thankful that he never robbed me before. I am thankful that although he took my wallet, he did not take my life. Although he took all I had, it was not much. And I am glad that it was I who was robbed, not I who did the robbing." Read Psalm 66:16–20, and consider the previous illustration. What does it teach you?

Shoes and Souls

The great gifts from the world are still insignificant compared to the incredible worth of one soul.

Mike shared two scriptures in this section: Mark 8:36 and Romans 10:9. What do they teach you? In comparison to the gifts the world has, what is the gift that God offers you through His only Son, Jesus? Have you received this gift? If you said the prayer Mike provided and asked Jesus into your heart, please share this great news with someone. You will find Mike's e-mail address in the final pages of this book. Let him know your decision. He will be thrilled to talk with you about it.

Drama Class

Only when a person takes off the mask
covering the heart will he finally be able to
play his true part in the drama of life.

Have you ever met an actor? What did you say? Mike described Mrs. Vaughn, a character actor from a TV show. How did she help Mike feel more confident? Who is in your life right now that makes you feel this way? Proverbs 12:25 provides a principle about kindness. What is it? Are you willing to show kindness to others?

The Medal

It is not the medal on the chest but the mettle in your character that develops you into a person of confidence.

Mike described an award that he was to receive from his drama teacher, Mrs. Vaughn. What was it? What were the words from Mrs. Vaughn that meant more to Mike than the medal? Do you agree with Mike that God knows what and who you need in life? Read Philippians 4:19 and Romans 8:28, and compare the two. Do you believe that God will do this for you? Why or why not?

CHAPTER 8

Pieces of Training

SYMPATHY

It was Friday afternoon, my last day at good old Hoxie High. I would be leaving on Monday for Fort Polk, Louisiana. I had joined the Army National Guard while still in high school and now I needed to complete basic training and advanced infantry training (AIT). I'd been in school for twelve years. Now Uncle Sam required seventeen weeks of my life for training and six additional years to complete my enlistment in the National Guard. I was already having second thoughts, but I knew it was too late. Once I placed my signature on the dotted line it was a done deal.

I was sitting in history class, pondering what the next few months would be like, when I saw someone walk past the door. The person looked like my dad, but he had never come to school, not even to watch me play ball. As I sat in class with my eyes fixed on the door, I had almost convinced myself it was not him—and then there he was in living color, knocking on the door. I was almost in a panic mode. My teacher went to the classroom door, and after a short conversation she turned to me and said, "Mike, you have a visitor."

I walked into the hall, where Dad was standing. I walked as far from the open door as possible to keep the other students from hearing our conversation. I said, "Dad, what's wrong?"

"Nothing is wrong," he replied. "I'm here to take you to lunch."

I could smell whiskey on his breath. It was an odor I hated, but I had smelled it enough to fully recognize the scent. I said, "Dad, I can't go to lunch with you. I only get thirty minutes, and there's just not enough time."

"I'll sign you out," he said, "and you don't have to come back to school today."

"No, Dad. This is my last day of school, and I want to be here. Besides, I have a job working in the lunchroom, and I can't leave them shorthanded."

He laughed and said, "They can make it without you." He was correct, but there was something down deep inside me that said, *Don't leave the school grounds with him.* I could feel the perspiration building under my Hoxie High School sweatshirt. Somehow, I found the courage to say, "I can't go with you, Dad."

He was visibly upset with me, and I could feel the tension building between us. "Are you coming with me or not?" he asked. His face was like stone, and his eyes were bloodshot.

At that moment I was at a loss for words. We just stared at each other for what seemed like eternity. I finally mustered the nerve to answer him. "I can't go, Dad. I'm sorry. I just can't."

He turned away from me and, without looking in my direction, he said, "I came by today to tell you I am dying." He paused, probably thinking I would respond, but I didn't say a word. "I only have a few months left to live." Again, I did not respond. He continued. "I was going to leave you my car, but now, I'm not leaving you one [blankety-blank] thing." He used some pretty choice words to describe what a terrible son I was.

I just looked at him as he walked away. I hated treating him that way, but I felt led not to get into his car. Dad was always so unpredictable; I just never knew what to expect from him. This was not the first time he'd told the dying story to gain sympathy. He used the same story when he tried to persuade Mother to let him come back home.

CLEAR HEAD

I went back to class and finished my last day. By the time the last bell rang, all I could think was, *School is out.* I had completed a new piece to add to my life puzzle. After school, several of us guys went to a friend's house to play basketball. We knew very well this might be our last chance to hang out together. After about an hour or so, I called home to tell Mother I was on my way. Mom answered the telephone, but before I could say anything, she screamed, "Don't come home! Your dad has a gun!"

I said, "Mom!" Suddenly, Dad was on the extension and ordered me to come home. I didn't say a word. I could hear him breathing on the other end, so I hung up. I called a family friend with whom we attended church; he was an

Arkansas state trooper. I didn't know what to do, so I shared the entire story with him. He took the telephone number I was calling from and told me to stay put until I got a call from either him or Mother.

I found out later that Dad had gone by our house after school, knowing all the kids would be home. He called Tony and asked him to come by the house to visit. Dad knew Mom would be home as soon as she got off work. Dad had a plan, and he executed it flawlessly. He had gathered the whole family together, except for me. After a short visit, Tony announced he needed to go home. At that point, Dad pulled a gun from his pocket and told Tony to have a seat. He explained, "We will wait for Mike to come home, and then I plan to kill all of you and then kill myself."

Our friend, the state trooper, rang the house number, and Dad answered the phone, probably thinking I was calling back. The trooper said, "Fred, I know what you are doing, and I am only ten minutes away. If you're there when I arrive, I will arrest you and take you to jail. You will be in serious trouble. I suggest you do yourself a favor and leave immediately."

Dad never wanted other people to be involved in his antics. He took the advice; Mother said he just walked out the front door without saying a word.

I am thankful God gave me a clear mind that day and that I did not leave the school grounds with Dad. I'm also thankful I did not go straight home after school. Maybe it was just another one of Dad's stunts, but maybe not. All I know is God was merciful to our family. He spread forth His hand of protection, and no one was hurt or killed.

BASIC TRAINING

Trying to filter through all the what-ifs can make you crazy. Like all the other episodes with Dad, our family had to accept it as reality, thank God for His protection, and move forward with our lives. For me, Monday morning came quickly, and before I could sort through all that had happened, I found myself on a bus heading to Fort Polk, Louisiana, for basic training.

At one point the bus driver stopped for a bathroom break, and I bought a Dr. Pepper. I unwrapped the tuna fish sandwich Mother had made for my trip, and the entire bus was filled with the delightful aroma of tuna. I'm sure the other passengers enjoyed the scent. With every bite, I thought of all the hamburgers Mom had fried for me at midnight and all those long talks and laughs we had shared. I could feel my eyes getting moist, and I remembered Mother telling me, "If a man's eyes don't leak, his head will swell." Mother had some funny sayings, but the older I got, the more sense they made.

We arrived at the reception station, and I was assigned to Bravo Company for eight weeks of what I refer to as *swamp training*. It was hard but not so much for an eighteen-year-old. I had attended football practices that were much more grueling. I enjoyed the physical part of the training but felt bad for the older guys who were not as physically fit. The drill sergeant had two goals: (1) to get everyone in shape for a tour in Vietnam; and (2) to train us well so we could stay alive. There was no difference in the training. It didn't matter whether we were National Guard (NG) or regular army (RA); the training was the same. There was a difference, however, in our minds. I knew I was going home after the training, but the boys who had been drafted knew they were going on a nine-month tour, perhaps placing them in harm's way.

Ringing Ears

I finished the eight-week basic training, and at that point I began my AIT classes. This was nine weeks of a specialized training, depending on one's military occupational skill (MOS). Mine was training as a gunner on an 81mm mortar. Once again, God was guiding my fate, but I could not then see what He was doing.

One day while training in the field, we were firing mortar rounds. I was the gunner, and another man was holding the shell. My earplugs were pulled out so I could hear the forward observer (FO) call the elevation for the round. I was supposed to set the elevation, insert my earplugs, and give the order to fire. Unfortunately, the man holding the shell let the round slip before I gave the order to fire, so my earplugs were not inserted. My head was so close to the barrel when the round exploded that I lost my equilibrium and fell to the ground. I tried to get up but again fell to the ground. I had no sense of balance.

The drill sergeant was quickly on the scene. I could hear a muffled sound coming from his mouth. When I looked at him, I could tell he was screaming at the top of his lungs. I tried to get up but couldn't stand. The ringing in my ears was so loud that I thought I had burst my eardrums. I felt the sergeant kick me on my leg and barely heard him say, "Get up! You are not getting out of this man's army." He had no idea I was National Guard. For all he knew, I was regular army and faking an injury.

I somehow managed to stagger to my feet, but the ringing was so loud I could hardly hear what was being said. Being young, I did not want to bring negative attention to myself, so I did not report the injury. I have lived with the results of that accident all my adult life. I didn't understand that God would use what had happened to add a piece to my life puzzle, and that would one day change the direction of my lifelong career.

I completed my training and arrived home, where I served all six years of my National Guard obligation.

JOB APPLICATION

When I arrived home from training I immediately began looking for employment. Living in a small town, jobs were hard to find, and good jobs paying a decent wage were almost nonexistent. After several weeks, I went to work for a local golf bag factory. It offered low wages, long hours, and few benefits, but it was the only job I could find. I worked there for around six months. One day the foreman introduced me to a new employee—a fellow with whom I had gone to school. I remembered that he had dropped out before graduating.

All day I pondered what I needed to do. Should I stay with what I deemed a dead-end job, or should I quit and start looking for something that paid a decent wage? I decided to look for something better. I quit my job that afternoon.

When I arrived home, I told Mother the whole story. I explained how much I disliked that job and that I felt there must be better opportunities in the marketplace. Mother was quite upset with me. She said, "Young man, you don't quit a job until you have another one." Normally, I would agree with that philosophy, but the problem was that while working at that job, I had no time to look for something better. In my mind, I had no choice but to quit; that is, if I wanted to better myself.

As I lay in bed that night, I remembered the many times I'd talked with God about my future when I was a boy. I found myself asking again for His help. I knew this time would eventually come, and now I desperately needed God's help to find a good job. I have always believed in being honest with God. He knows everything, so why not just confess? I discussed quitting my job and why I had left. Then I added, "Father, you know Mother is mad at me." I was hoping He would sense my urgency and move quickly to help me find a good job. God loves His children, and I believed He would provide me with a good-paying job.

I left the next day to look for employment in Jonesboro, located twenty-one miles from where we lived in Hoxie. A friend had mentioned to me that the General Electric plant was hiring. GE was the place where everyone wanted to work; that is, if you were looking for a factory-type job. I drove straight to the plant. It was huge, much larger than I'd imagined.

As I walked into the front office, the receptionist asked if she could help me.

"I'm looking for a job," I said. "Is GE hiring?"

"Yes, for the second shift," she said, "but all applications are accepted through the state Employment Security Division, located in the downtown area."

I thanked her and headed toward the employment office. When I arrived, the lobby was full of people. I stood in a long line, trying to make my way to the front desk. I talked with some of the people in line and soon realized almost everyone was there for a different reason. Some people were signing up for unemployment, and others looking for different types of jobs. One man asked me about the type work I was seeking.

"I want to work at General Electric," I said.

He just chuckled and said, "Good luck." He seemed to imply that probably wasn't going to happen.

I finally made it to the front desk, where a young lady asked me how she could help.

"I'm looking for a job," I said. "I want to fill out an employment application for GE."

She handed me some paperwork to complete but said, "GE is not hiring."

I tried to explain what the receptionist at GE had told me, but she acted like I offended her by disputing what she'd said. I tried to smooth out our conversation by being overly nice to her, but it didn't work. I realized I had not made a friend, and she probably would not assist me with my goal. I took a seat with all the other folks and started filling out the mountain of paperwork she had given me, none of which referenced General Electric.

I looked around the room and saw people talking and laughing, and suddenly I felt alone and very insignificant. Those old thoughts of unworthiness started creeping in around me. At this point, I usually would have withdrawn into my shell and become very quiet, but instead, I started mentally praying. *Lord, please help me. Please show me what to do. I need a job, and I need your help.* I blocked out the noise in the room and completed the paperwork. I sat there in the lobby, knowing if I took the paperwork back to the young lady at the front desk I would walk out with no job. Sometimes you just need to wait on the Lord, and that's what I did. I waited for Him to help me.

HIRED

I remembered the story Mother had told me about the two men—one who was successful and the other, because of his shyness, who was not. I continued my talk with God, mentally saying, *Lord, I need Your help. Please show me what to do.*

I sat in the lobby for a least an hour. I thought, *If I leave, I will go home with no job, and that was unacceptable.* I kept my eyes on the front desk and noticed the young lady's chair was not occupied. I slowly got up from my seat and walked forward, but for some reason, I didn't stop at the reception desk. Instead, I walked around it and into the main area, where there were many offices. I spotted an office with a name above the door: "Mrs. Kafka." I walked by slowly and saw a middle-aged woman shuffling through a stack of papers. She was alone, so I knocked on the open door. She looked up and, with a big smile, asked if I needed help.

I said, "Ma'am, I just returned home from the military, and I am looking for a job." I explained I wanted to work for General Electric and that I'd been told they were hiring.

She said, "Come in. I interview applicants for GE, so you have come to the right place."

My mind was racing so fast I questioned whether I'd heard her correctly. As I sat down, I handed her my paperwork.

"Why do you want to work in a factory?" she asked.

"Everyone knows GE isn't like most factories," I answered. "They offer great benefits and good pay. If I was fortunate enough to get a job with them, I would work just as hard as I worked on the farm, and they would never be sorry they hired me."

"Would you be willing to work the night shift?"

"I will work any shift," I said.

She wrote something on a small piece of paper, and, with a smile, she handed the paper to me, saying, "Report to work at the main office this afternoon at 3:30."

Before I left her office, I hugged her and told her how grateful I was for her help.

She smiled and said, "I know you will work out just fine."

She had no idea that her hiring me was the answer to my prayer. On my way out, I walked by the young lady at the reception desk. She saw I was coming from one of the main offices and said, "Can I help you, sir?"

I said, "No thanks. I have already been helped. I just got a job working for GE."

MOVING MOMENTS

I walked on clouds all the way back to my car. I sat there for a long while, trying to soak in what had happened. I knew God had performed a miracle for me. I needed time to review everything in my mind. I needed to register the reality of all that had occurred. It was that day I realized that God is a personal God. He hears our requests and answers prayers, according to His will.

I have revisited that day in my mind many times, always remembering, with a grateful heart, a loving God who saw my need, heard my prayer, and provided for me in my despair. His hand was on my life in real time, moving me in the direction I needed to go to fulfill His overall will for my life. God added a piece to my life puzzle that day that eventually would open doors and change my life forever.

I worked for General Electric for the next six years. It was a good job, but as with any factory job, it was governed by supply and demand. That means there were times when I worked overtime and times when I was laid off. For me, it always seemed to be November, December, and January when work was scarce.

I knew Mother couldn't help me financially, and I would never have asked her for help. While laid off from GE, I had to find part-time work to pay my bills. I worked for Mayflower, a national moving company. They hired part-time workers and paid in cash, usually determined by how hard the employee worked. I also picked up work at a local produce plant. Eighteen-wheelers pulled in trailers full of potatoes in hundred-pound sacks. They needed young men with strong backs to unload those trailers. I somehow always survived until GE called me back to work.

During my sixth year of working for GE, I was approached by a representative of the AFL-CIO union, of which I was a member. They asked if I would be interested in interviewing for a state job. The job was Deputy Director of Labor and was appointed by the Arkansas governor. I agreed to interview, although I thought I didn't have a chance of getting the job. I was wrong.

I had been dating a girl from Florida who was in Arkansas attending Arkansas State University in Jonesboro. Shortly after her graduation, we were married. A few months later, I was offered the job with the Department of Labor, and we found ourselves moving to Little Rock, Arkansas.

My job as Deputy Director of Labor oversaw many branches of state government under our heading, one of which was the State Employment Security Division. On one of my road trips, I had the opportunity to revisit Mrs. Kafka. I gave my business card to the person at the reception desk and asked specifically for Helen Kafka. It had been over six years since the day she hired me for the job with GE. I was now dressed in a suit, and my business card identified me as Deputy Director of Labor. When she came out to greet me, I knew she didn't recognize me. I explained who I was and how she had helped me on that day so long ago. I told her how I had prayed for guidance while sitting in her office lobby and that I ultimately had been led to her. It was a very emotional and moving moment for us both.

CAREER CHANGE

When my job in Little Rock was over, my wife and I decided to move from Arkansas to begin a new life in Florida. We moved to Saint Petersburg, where my wife had grown up. She got a job as a schoolteacher, and I went to work for the city government.

While I was working in that job, I decided I wanted to

pursue a career with the Saint Petersburg Fire Department. I discussed this with one of my supervisors and was encouraged to move forward with that opportunity. I took the written test and the agility test and passed both with no problem. The day came for me to meet the fire chief and set a date to start my new career. There was one more thing, though, that was just preliminary and routine. It included an eye examination and hearing test. To my dismay, I failed the hearing test. When the mortar shell exploded next to my ear during my military training, it damaged my eardrum, taking away my ability to hear high frequencies—for example, a baby's cry. The fire chief expressed how sorry he was, but I did not meet the qualifications to work as a fireman.

I couldn't believe what had happened. I finally had decided upon a lifetime career, only to have it snatched away by a past freak accident.

I had made a serious miscalculation. I decided upon my lifetime career, but God had other plans in store for my life. As we often do, I forgot to consult God about my decision, and He was about to move me into an entirely different career. This one would include sales. Who would think that a boy nicknamed Mouse would ever make his living in sales? I am convinced; God does have a sense of humor.

QUESTIONS

On Monday morning, I went back to my old job. I was wearing a suit and tie, working in a job that looked impressive, but it didn't pay much money. I couldn't quite figure out why that freak accident had happened to me, taking away my chances, years later, to be a fireman. You might remember that I have never thought it wrong to ask God a question; it's only wrong to question God. I have always kept that thought in mind when talking with God about my life or, for that matter, about anything. I believe we should all speak softly, with the right amount of humility and respect, keeping in mind the great God we are addressing.

I have concluded that life has many pieces, and God uses them all to complete our life puzzles. Each piece offers great lessons, and our God is an excellent teacher. About the time we think we have everything figured out, God changes our direction. If I have learned anything about God, it is that I can always trust Him to do what is best for me. I may not always understand, but if I can just be still (Psalm 46:10; Exodus 14:13) long enough without doing something to mess up everything, God will reveal His plan. He is always far ahead of me and my thinking (Isaiah 55:8–9). I started attending church in Saint Petersburg. It was a wonderful church with a great pastor who preached straight from God's Word.

My wife's dad was a manager for a national food manufacturing company. He knew I was looking for a career job and asked me if I wanted to be an independent distributor, selling products his company manufactured. When I asked him to explain the job, he said I would be self-employed. "You'll have to have your own truck, buy products that come in weekly, settle your account on time, and manage your own business. If you work hard, you could make good money, but if you don't work hard or manage your business properly, you won't do well."

I signed a distributor agreement to be an independent

contractor and started with a large outlined geographical territory but my space in the supermarkets was limited, consequently my sales were low. Within the first six months after I started, the grocery stores expanded my space, and my business doubled. By the end of my first year, I was making more money than I had ever made in my life. It turned out to be a great opportunity, and I owe MR. John Davis for giving me that chance. It involved long hours, sometimes fourteen or fifteen hours every day, but I did not mind the hard work. My main concern was making a good living for my family. I remembered my prayer as a boy, when I told God I had no desire to be rich but asked Him to help me obtain a good-paying job. I'd promised God I would work hard and make Him proud. He has always answered my prayer, and I have always worked diligently to fulfill my promise to Him.

HIS VOICE

Every morning I stopped at the same service station to fill the gas tank in my business truck. A service station attendant named John worked there, and he usually walked over to talk as I pumped my gas. John had a club foot, and he explained how difficult it was to be on his feet all day. Knowing his story, I always appreciated the effort he made to walk those extra steps across the station lot just to visit with me.

I had placed a hundred-dollar bill in the back of my wallet. It was my little piece of money to spend as I pleased. One morning as I pulled into the station, God spoke to my heart and told me to give John the hundred-dollar bill. This had never happened to me, where God spoke directly to my heart about an issue. I had helped people in need by giving money, but this was different, and I knew it was different. Someone I respected once told me that people would use me and that I should not be so free to hand out money. With those words ringing in my ears, I dismissed God's voice. I filled my truck with gasoline, and later that day I broke the hundred-dollar bill, tucking sixty dollars back in my wallet.

The next morning, I pulled into the service station to fill up. I had not given a second thought to God's request to give the money to John. Immediately as I shut off the engine, God spoke to my heart: *"Take the sixty dollars out of your wallet and give it to John."* I was so overwhelmed that I spoke these words out loud: "Lord, if John comes over, I will give him the money."

There came John, with a smile on his face. As he arrived at my side, I didn't wait. I just pulled out the money and tucked it into his shirt pocket. I said, "John, I'm not sure why, but I feel led to give you this money."

John touched his shirt pocket without looking at the money and said, "Mike, I came over to say good-bye. I was saved two weeks ago at a small church around the corner, and God told me to go home to Georgia to be with my wife and baby girl. This money means a lot. Thank you!"

I was stunned but tried not to give away my emotions. We said our good-byes, and I got back into my truck. My tears were falling to the point that I couldn't see to drive. I blurted out, "God, I am so sorry that I didn't give John all of the money you told me to give." God spoke clearly to my heart, saying, *"Don't worry. I'll take care of John, but now you know my voice, and you will never forget it."* God has subsequently spoken to my heart many times over the years, and I have learned to move quickly to do whatever He instructs me to do.

You may think it peculiar that I talk of God speaking to my heart. If so, I hope you will reconsider your feelings concerning these matters. I believe this is a gift God gives to whomever He chooses.

I look forward to seeing John again someday, only next time he will not be dragging his foot. What a great God, who will heal us all someday.

8

Life Lessons: Pieces of Training

In our lives, we will undergo different training programs and opportunities. We volunteer for some, while for others we are "volun-told." Personal and professional training helps us in the long run, with the promotions and financial increases. Spiritual training to listen to the voice of God, however, will do more than simply make us successful in our jobs. This heart-impacting process will help us to become faithful in our spiritual service. Consider these lessons and ask yourself, "Do I feel like I am ready to train?"

Sympathy

Fooling the hearts of others, in the end,
will only make you the fool.

What is the difference between sympathy and empathy? Sympathy, like pity, is what one feels for a person. Empathy is what you feel *with* the person. They both intersect with our personal feelings. Mike mentioned two times when he had a feeling about not going with his dad. Do you think Mike remembered his mother's example of standing up to his father? Have you ever had to stand up to someone? What was the situation, and what did you do? In Psalm 56:3–4 is a wonderful promise that helps us to stand up for ourselves, even when it is tough. What does the verse mean to you?

Clear Head

Courage is more than rushing in; it is also reaching out.

What does it mean to be courageous? Movies have depicted it, and books have discussed it, but what does the Bible say about it? In 2 Timothy 1:6–7, the apostle Paul writes of how we can be courageous. Read the passage and write down some benefits of courage. How will these help you in your life? Mike described a very scary situation with his dad. How did he handle it? What would you have done? Read Psalm 27:1. How can your prayer be the first step of courage?

Basic Training

The best training you can ever receive is not the one that prepares you for war but one that prepares you for life.

Mike described his transition from high school to the military. What were some memories he reflected on during the trip to basic training? Why are memories like these important to you during a time of transition? In Chronicles 28:20, David reminds his son, Solomon, about some important principles needed for Solomon's transition from a youth to a man. What were they? What do these childhood memories mean to you today?

Ringing Ears

Only when the silence of a need is broken can the deaf ears of humanity finally hear and respond.

Mike described an accident that caused permanent damage. What was it? Why did Mike not report it? Have you ever suffered something that impacted you physically, emotionally, or mentally, and you didn't report it? Mike lived with the results of the accident all his life. What are your "ringing ear" results? As you read Isaiah 41:10–13, take a moment to write down some of God's help for our damaging experiences.

Job Application

In order for us to grasp something better,
we have to be willing to first empty
our hands of what we have.

Have you ever filled out a job application? What type of job was it? Mike wanted a job with opportunities for the future. Where did he want to work? What was he willing to do to get the position? What would you do for the job you wanted? During the paperwork process, Mike took the time to pray. Why? Would you have stopped to pray? In Ephesians 6:18, we are encouraged to "Pray at all times." Why does prayer help us with the directions we go in life? How has it helped you?

Hired

The threshold of a door and an opportunity are similar
in that both require a step forward to enter it.

Do you recall the story that Mike's mom told him about the successful man and the shy man? How did this illustration help Mike land the job he wanted with General Electric? Would you have waited as Mike did? Why? Read Nehemiah 2:2–5. What can you learn from this scripture about not being afraid to step out in faith?

Moving Moments

Taking a chance can make you feel lucky.
Having someone give you a chance
can make you feel blessed.

Mike described the variety of part-time jobs he held during his time with GE. What job did he attain that opened the door for him to reconnect with Mrs. Kafka? Why did Mike go to see her? What does it mean for someone to give you a chance at something? Has someone done this for you? Read Philippians 1:3–4. God gives us a chance to say thank you. Who do you need to thank today?

Career Change

A job is what you do for life. A career
is who you become in living.

Have you ever wanted something that you could not have? What was it, and how did you handle not getting it? Mike wanted a career in firefighting. Why could he not get the job? What happened when this first career did not work out for him? Psalm 37:5 provides a step in finding the right career for your future. What is that step? Are you willing to trust God to do it?

Questions

The answer to the question you have is not in the just the question but in the reason behind asking it.

What do you think about Mike's statement, "I have never thought it wrong to ask God a question; it's only wrong to question God"? Which one do you normally do, and why? Take a moment and compare Psalm 118:8; Psalm 46:10; Exodus 14:13; and Isaiah 55:8–9. Mike referred to those verses. What does it mean to be still and trust that God has a perfect plan for your life? How will this impact the way you look at a career?

His Voice

A baby never wonders if the mom can hear his voice. We should never wonder if God hears our voices. We should wonder if we truly hear His.

Take a moment to read John 10:1–6. Mike spoke about a gas station worker named John. What did John do that caught Mike's attention? Mike was impressed by God to do something for John. What happened? Have you ever had an experience like this? What happened? How can we know God's voice in our lives?

CHAPTER 9

Pieces of Transformation

LITTLE RED WAGON

I continued to run my distributorship, and God continued to bless us financially and many other ways. I loved the small church I attended, and I met privately with the pastor from time to time. There were questions I needed answered, and Pastor Tyace was a very patient man. He answered many of my questions and taught me about loving and serving God. You may remember my inquisitive nature as a boy, living in the Blue House. God had rekindled that nature, and now, thirty years later, many of my questions concern God Himself.

I am thankful for Christians who take time to minister to young men and women. Many young people desire to serve God but need encouragement and guidance. Perhaps you are someone who serves in this capacity. If so, thank you for your investment, and may God bless you.

My wife and I bought a small, two-bedroom, one-bathroom house with a den. It wasn't fancy, but because it was our first house, we loved it. It was a perfect little house to start our family, and that's exactly what we did. Our son, Steven Michael, was born on June 18, 1979, and soon became the joy of our lives.

There was a small park in our neighborhood that Steve and I loved to visit in the afternoons and weekends. I bought Steve a little red wagon and assembled it myself. I'm not mechanically inclined, and I mistakenly installed the tongue of the wagon backward. Steve loved the wagon and didn't realize Dad's mistake. Others were quick to point it out, though, but in my resolve, I decided to leave the wagon as it was. As Steve grew up, we often laughed about his having the only wagon of its kind in the neighborhood.

We used his new method of transportation to make our rounds—first, to the park to play on the swings, and then, to a little ice cream shop at the end of our block. We would sit on the curb at the back of the shop and enjoy our ice cream cones. We laughed and talked away many special hours. It reminded me of the question-and-answer days I spent with my mother back in the Blue House. These were special pieces to my life puzzle. I loved creating them with Steve. He was the joy of my life then and still is today.

TIMETABLE

As my business continued to grow, we decided to build a new house. The house was bigger but not necessarily better. There was no park for Steve and me to enjoy. I started coaching T-ball with a friend, Frank Trump. Steve was just old enough to play, and Frank had a daughter, Shelly, who played on our team. We enjoyed coaching, probably more than the youngsters enjoyed playing. Frank passed away much too young; I miss talking with my friend.

After several years of working as an independent distributor, I was offered a job as a district manager for a national baking company. I turned down the offer several times because it required that our family move to another city. Finally, I decided to take the job, and we moved to Jacksonville, Florida.

I worked for a regional manager named Don Williamson. Don was a great man to work for, and over time we became close friends. We would talk about everything, and because religion was my favorite topic, it eventually became part of our conversation. Don asked questions about what I believed, and I always tried to answer him from a biblical perspective. I worked with Don for almost six years. During those years, he never made a firm commitment of faith.

As Christians, we cannot save anyone, but we are obligated to share our faith, and that's what I did with Don. There are two things I firmly believe: (1) God does not work on our timetable, and (2) He is not willing for anyone to be lost. I believed God had a plan for Don. I just needed to be patient, which I will admit is sometimes difficult for me to do.

BIGGER AND BETTER

After working as a district manager for about two years, Don sent me to a training meeting held at our corporate office. While at the meeting, I shared a room with a district manager from Miami named Abe. After the second day of training classes, Abe told me he had not been trained to do many of the tasks we were discussing in classes.

I said, "Abe, we will be here for a week. If you want to learn some of these skills, I can teach you at night after the training day is complete."

He made a statement that took me completely off guard. "You know I am a Jew."

"No, I didn't know that," I responded.

"I am a Cuban Jew, and I know you are a Christian. Christians hate Jews, so why would you help me?"

"Abe, Christians don't hate Jews. Why would you ever say something like that?"

"You blame us for killing your Jesus," he said.

"Abe Christians do not blame Jews for the death of our Savior," I told him. "We blame ourselves. Jesus was a Jew. How could I ever hate you for being a Jew?"

We did not speak of that topic again, but throughout that week we spent our nights reviewing the responsibilities of his job as a district manager. He was quick to learn and a very intelligent man. When the week was over, we parted as good friends, not knowing when or if we would ever work together again. I couldn't help but think that God put me and Abe together for a reason. I have learned that God is always working to fulfill His overall plans, and they are usually bigger and better than any one of us could imagine. God had His plan for Abe, and He had a plan for me. I just needed to remember, "Patience is a virtue saith the Lord."

PARTY OF ONE

One day, Don, my regional manager, told me he was going to send me to Chattanooga, Tennessee, with six other district managers from across the country. He said our job was to work for two weeks in towns located geographically around our corporate office. We were to make the markets shine, gain space, and place new rack fixtures on which to place our products throughout the markets. All six district managers flew in and gathered one afternoon at the corporate office to receive our assignments. This is where I first met Mark Foster, who has become a lifelong friend and a man I greatly admire for his unfaltering friendship and his vast knowledge of our business.

We hit the market early the next morning and started making notes of needed improvements. We immediately began ordering and placing racks. Although the work was hard and the days were long, the market really started looking great. By the end of the two weeks, we had completed our goals, and it was time to go back to our districts.

On the last night before returning home, we all gathered in my hotel room just to talk, relax, and say our good-byes. One of the managers suggested we each throw twenty dollars into a pot and use the money to buy some alcohol for a last-night bash. I sat quietly as the party was planned and everyone put their money on the bed—all except for me. It was not fun being the only holdout, but I knew I couldn't be part of the plan.

One of the guys I regard as my friend noticed that I hadn't

put my money on the bed. He turned to me and, in front of everyone, said, "Mike, put your money in."

I said, "Guys, you know we are not supposed to haul alcohol in a company car. If you get caught, you could lose your jobs. You do what you will, but I am not going to be part of this."

One of the guys replied, "Just put your money in. You don't have to do any drinking. By putting your money in, we will know that you won't say anything about the party."

"My lips are sealed," I said.

He frowned. "That's not good enough; you should put your money in."

I looked him straight in the eyes because I didn't want him to misunderstand my determination. I said, "My friend, I have been browbeaten by better men than you."

We left the next morning to return to our districts. Years later, one of the district managers who'd been present in the room told me he wished he had also said no to the party.

"It wasn't a pleasant experience to take a stand against what I knew would be an unpopular decision," I told him. "I know some guys in the room will never understand why I took that stand, but I can't live my life for them. I could have explained in more detail, but it probably wouldn't have made any difference."

We all have decisions to make in life, and many of those decisions need to be made long before we find ourselves in tough spots. My decision to never drink alcohol was made as a child, and I intend to keep my promise.

GAME OF TWENTY-ONE

My job as a district manager became more involved as time passed. There were several corporate headquarter calls that were very time-consuming—for example, those regarding Publix, Winn-Dixie, Naval Air Station Jacksonville, and other companies; seven all together—as well as there being ten independent distributors in my district. Food Lion was building stores as fast as they could buy the land to build. I sometimes had as many as nine store sets during one week. Store sets are when vendors from various companies work for retailers to re-align and stock grocery shelves. If you don't show up to work your products are usually left out of the supermarket in-line space.

One day I arrived home after a grueling day and was faced with a mountain of paperwork. As I walked into the house, Steve, now around twelve years old, was standing by the door with his basketball in his hand. He said, "Dad, do you want to play some Twenty-One?"

"Bud, I can't," I said, using the nickname I often called Steve. "I have so much work to do."

I saw his little face drop with disappointment. I loved my son, and the words I spoke about being too busy to spend time with him hurt me to my core. I walked into my office and sat down at my desk. It was at that moment I made another promise to myself. I promised I would never give up the most important part of being a dad, not for a few extra hours of paperwork. I walked back into the den, where Steve was still holding the basketball in his hand. and said, "Bud, you better get warmed up. I'm fixing to put a whupping on you as soon as I change clothes."

After that day, Steve often waited for me to get home, and his basketball was never far away. I think back on those days and am thankful for the many hours he and I spent on the court. Steve grew up, and I had to resort to making some serious fouls on the basketball court, just to keep up with the boy. I miss those days of playing ball with Steve. Those pieces of my life puzzle flew by much too fast, but you know, I don't miss that paperwork one bit.

THE PICTURE

My mother was having some serious issues with her health, and I decided to fly home to visit with her. I flew to Memphis, Tennessee, and rented a car. I drove the sixty-five miles, through Memphis, over the Memphis/Arkansas Bridge into Arkansas, and onward to Mother's house. Mom and I sat up late that first night, into the early morning hours. Because of Mother's poor health, my brother Byron recently had told me that he and his wife, Tammy, might have to move into her house to take care of her.

Mom wanted to talk about God, specifically heaven. She asked me to tell her everything I knew about heaven. We talked about the beauty and the reunions with loved ones. Through our tears, I learned what was on Mother's mind. She never brought up the issue of dying, but it was obvious to me where her mind was focused.

While I was home, I decided to drive to Paragould, Arkansas, to visit my Grandmother Simmons. Dad was living with Grandmother, and I would be able to visit with them both at the same time. Dad was an avid artist who loved painting. He would paint beautiful pictures on canvas using oil paint. When I arrived at Grandmother's house, I noticed that Dad had lined up ten of his paintings in the living room. I said, "Dad, you've been busy painting."

"Yes, and I painted one of those pictures especially for you," he said.

"Which one?"

In response, he just laughed, looked at Grandmother with a smile, and said to me, "Which one do you like the best?"

I walked over to the paintings and placed my hand on an oil painting of a ship on a rough sea. The ship was being tossed about furiously. I said, "This is the one I like the most."

Dad smiled. "That's the one I painted for you."

"Dad, it's beautiful. Are you sure you want me to have it?"

He said again, "Yes, I painted it for you." I could sense the joy in his voice that I had selected the correct painting. Dad explained, "Son, the ship is me, and the waves throwing the ship from side to side represent my life."

My heart was tender toward Dad because I knew what he'd said was true. He was such a talented man, but because of his excessive drinking he'd either lost or hurt everyone he held dear.

SENSE OF RELIEF

Grandmother asked if I would help her to the bedroom; she wanted to lie down. I helped her to bed, where we visited for just a little while. I kissed her good-bye and told her how much I loved her. I walked back into the living room and told Dad I needed to get back to Mother's house. I picked up my painting, and Dad walked with me to my car. I placed the painting into the trunk, and as I turned around, Dad was standing on the curb with his head bowed. I walked over and touched his arm. Without looking up he said, "Son, I know I have mistreated you kids and Kathleen [my mother]. Do you think you will ever be able to forgive me for all I have done?"

I lifted his chin, and as his eyes met mine, I said, "Dad, I forgave you a long time ago."

I'll never forget the expression on his face. It changed instantly from sadness to a sense of relief. It was as though I had given him the answer to a question that had haunted him for years. Dad looked as though the weight of the world had been lifted from him. We embraced each other but did not speak, as the hug said all the words that needed to be spoken. I will never forget how Dad lay his head on my shoulder in his effort to savor the moment. I can't remember Dad ever hugging me before, but in that moment, God allowed a father and son to finally be reconciled.

I drove away that day not realizing I would never see Dad or Grandmother on this earth again. Grandmother Simmons passed away first, but I was not able to attend her funeral. A few months later, Dad died. My brother Byron called with the news. Dad had been attending a church close to where they lived and had accepted the Lord as his Savior. I can't help but wonder if our conversation that day had something to do with Dad's making his decision to surrender his heart to the Lord.

I am so very glad that after all the terrible stories I have written about Dad I can end this chapter on a positive note.

Dad wasted a big part of his life, but God, in His mercy, saved Dad before his death. I know one day we will spend quality time together, to which there will be no end. When I look at Dad's painting, I believe the sea is now calm. There is a pastor, Bill Bailey, who made a statement during one of his sermons that gave me great comfort. He said, "There are no big I's or little yous at the foot of the cross." That is so very true; we are all saved sinners.

REGIONAL MANAGER

About two years passed, and I was offered the job as a regional manager in the Tampa Bay area. Geographically, the region took in Tampa to Miami, and Miami to Orlando and everything in between. We moved back to Saint Petersburg, where I was on the road traveling, usually from Monday to Thursday, with calls all day Friday. Ironically, Abe, the friend I had made over three years before at the meeting in Chattanooga, was a district manager in Miami, and now he worked for me. My new job required my full attention, and soon my wife and I were divorced. As you may know, there are no winners in a divorce.

As time went by, I continued with my job responsibilities, spending a great deal of time traveling throughout the South Florida market, which offered the most sales growth opportunities. Abe was now my main district manager in the Miami–Hialeah market. The training I offered Abe had come full circle, and his ability to speak Spanish was instrumental in the South Florida growth.

As time passed, I met a beautiful lady named Jenny, and

soon we were married and began our life together in Plant City, Florida. Jenny had one son, Melvin, who had a beautiful wife, Frances. We have two sweet and talented grandchildren by them: Morgan, whom I lovingly call Missy, and Kyle. God has blessed our family.

Before Jenny and I got married, she asked me to promise her we would attend church and serve God. I made that promise to God and Jenny and fully intended to keep my promise. We started attending the First Baptist Church in Plant City, where, at that time, Dr. Ron Churchill was the senior pastor. I met with Pastor Ron and asked him if I could be baptized again. He told me I didn't need to go through that process if I had previously been baptized. I asked him if he would allow me that privilege, since I wanted to rededicate my life, and he agreed.

He gave me a date to be baptized, and I wrote it on my calendar. The time came, and Jenny and I told friends I was going to be baptized that morning. When I arrived at the baptismal area, Pastor Ron asked me why I was there. I said, "To get baptized."

He informed me it was scheduled for the next week. I couldn't wait to get home to check my calendar to see if I was wrong about the date. I was always very punctual, and there it was. I was correct about the date—at least the date I had entered on my calendar.

Precious Cargo

The next week I went to be baptized. While changing clothes, so I could be submerged in water baptism, I overheard the pastor having a conversation with some folks. He asked if their little boy, "who was around the age of 8," could walk by himself down the stairs into the water to be baptized; they said no, he could not because of his illness. Pastor Ron told them he could not physically carry the boy down the stairs, baptize him, and then carry him up the stairs.

I walked out of my dressing area and said, "I can do that for you guys."

Pastor Ron said, "You think you can hold him while I baptize him?"

I nodded. "I know I can. I have worked out all of my life for such a time as this."

While further pondering the confusion regarding my baptism date, I now believe God placed me there on that Sunday morning (instead of the previous week) to assist with baptizing this little boy. When the time came, I picked him up and carried him down the stairs, where Pastor Ron baptized him. As he came up from the water, he raised his hands over his head and the whole church erupted in applause. It was a glorious thing to behold. I was blessed that God and Pastor Ron had allowed me to take part in that amazing event. I was especially moved when, a few years later, because of his illness, the little boy went to be with the Lord. I cherish that baptism, as it was the first opportunity God gave me to serve Him since the rededication of my life.

GREATEST DAY

Jenny and I started attending a Sunday school class. Our teacher's name was Dub, and he was an excellent teacher. I loved his class and was always disappointed whenever he had to miss a Sunday.

After a Sunday church service Jenny and I were talking, and I told her I felt I had failed Steve because I hadn't taken him to Sunday school and church when he was growing up. It wasn't that I hadn't wanted to, but certain circumstances prevented me from doing so. "I told Jenny, I had been praying and asking God to help me know how to approach my son," I explained that. One morning, during my prayer time, I was talking with the Lord about Steve and God spoke plainly to my heart. It was the same voice that had spoken to me about John and giving him money. He said, *"I will give you back the years the locusts have eaten."* I didn't quite know how to digest those words. I didn't understand what God meant, but I knew the words were spoken to my heart from God.

A few weeks later, on Friday afternoon, Steve called from the University of Central Florida to say he was coming to spend the weekend. As usual, we were thrilled to have him. Jenny has always loved and treated Steve like her own son, and she cooked a great meal. We talked and laughed, and Steve filled us in on stories from college, one of which was about a party he had attended.

"Was there a chaperone?" I asked.

He laughed. "I'm an adult," he said. "I don't need a chaperone.

We cleaned up the dishes and turned on the television. About 9:00 p.m., Jenny announced she was going to bed to read. Immediately, the Holy Spirit spoke to my heart and said, *"Turn off the TV, and talk with Steve."* I knew what I was being told to do, and I did it. After turning off the TV, I said, "Son, come over here on the couch. I need to talk with you about something."

When he was settled next to me, I said, "Tonight you told me several times that you are an adult, and I believe you are correct. Being an adult comes with a great number of responsibilities, one of which includes deciding the way you choose to live as an adult."

Steve and I talked about a great number of things, including committing one's life to God. We discussed the plan of salvation and what it means to follow Christ. I asked Steve if he believed the things we had discussed, and he said he did. I asked him to pray with me. He reached out his hand, and we asked the Lord to forgive and come into his life to live forever.

Thinking back, that was the most rewarding day of my adult life—to be able to pray that prayer with my very own son. God had given me back all the years the locusts had eaten, and, with a grateful heart, I fully understood what God had done. Steve and I went to our bedrooms; I couldn't wait to wake Jenny to tell her everything God had done.

The next week, I told Jenny I needed to talk to Steve about being baptized. A couple of days later, Steve called me and asked, "Dad, am I supposed to be baptized?"

I said, "Yes, you are. I will talk with Pastor Ron and arrange it." Two weeks later Steve came home, and Pastor Ron baptized him. Steve came up from the water and walked-up the stairs, where I was waiting with open arms.

He said, "Dad, I'm soaked."

"I don't care." I hugged him, knowing that what he had done—accepting Christ—was going to add the most important piece to Steve's life puzzle. I knew his decision would change the course of his entire life. I was excited for Steve, proud of him for making his decision at such a young age, and grateful to God for giving me back the years the locusts had eaten. God takes an interest in our lives and He loves to answer our prayers.

Steve graduated UCF with a master's degree in information systems. He married a beautiful and talented young lady from Waterford, Connecticut, Kristina Yacovou. Jenny and I have two beautiful grandchildren by them, Michael and Matthew, and as of this writing, they have another boy on the way. We love our children and our grandchildren; God has blessed us greatly.

COURAGE

On Fridays' I always received business calls from all my district managers. During Abe's, call he explained that he and his wife were coming to Orlando over the weekend and asked if they could visit with Jenny and me. We were excited to have them in our home, and our excitement intensified when Abe asked if they could attend church with us on Sunday. Over the years, I had spent many hours talking with Abe about my faith. He being of the Jewish faith, he had many questions, and I appreciated every one. Many times Abe would meet in my hotel room, and I would answer his questions using a Gideon Bible, which was always found in the hotel desk drawer.

Later in my life, Bob Shivers extended an invitation for me to become a member of the International Gideon

Society. I accepted his invitation and am a proud supporter and member of the Gideons today, working to help make God's Word available throughout the world.

After we all attended church together, we had lunch, and Abe and his wife both told us how much they enjoyed the main service and Sunday school. A few weeks later, I was working in Miami, and all Abe wanted to talk about was the church service they had attended. He asked me many questions concerning what had been taught. I answered all his questions and explained the full plan of salvation. He wanted to know if salvation was for everyone, including Jews. I told him it was available for anyone who would believe and place his faith in Jesus's death, burial, and resurrection. I also explained the meaning of a "messianic Jew." Simply put, this would be a Jewish person who had accepted Jesus as their Messiah. It does not change the fact that you are a Jew, you can still celebrate your Jewish culture.

Several weeks later, I returned to Miami.

I met Abe at the hotel in Hialeah. He was all smiles as he walked into my hotel room. "What are you up to?" I asked.

"I did it, I prayed to Jesus and asked Him to save me."

"Abe, that is wonderful. Did you tell your wife?"

"Yes, she prayed too."

Abe had two grown daughters who were educated in Jerusalem. I asked, "What did the girls say?"

He replied, "I didn't tell them."

I immediately realized the courage it had taken for Abe to make his commitment. It had been almost ten years since God had put Abe and me together, sharing the same hotel room. God used that time to soften a Jewish man's heart and eventually lead him to salvation's door. Abe opened that door. God uses people, places, and time to accomplish His overall will.

EULOGY

A year or so later, Abe retired. He called me one afternoon, and we made small talk. Then he asked for a favor. It caught me off guard when he asked if I would do his eulogy. Before I could ask any questions, he said, "Don't worry; I'm not dying."

We laughed, and I asked, "Why are you asking me to do this?"

He brushed it off, saying, "I was just thinking about who I would want to speak for me, and I want you to do me this favor."

"I'd be honored to do that for you."

Abe never shared anything with me about his health, but within a year, he passed away. His wife called to tell me he had died of cancer.

She called back that same day to give me his funeral arrangements. During the second call, she said, "Mike, I know Abe asked you to conduct a eulogy for him. The girls want to know if you can do that without mentioning the name of Jesus."

"I can't do that," I said.

"I was afraid you couldn't," she said. "You know we are Jewish, and Abe is a Jew, so we will ask someone else to speak. I hope you understand."

There were so many things I wanted to say, but I felt it was best to honor her request without rebuttal.

I attended the funeral of Abe, a man I deeply respected. He loved his wife and family very much. Through my friendship with Abe, I have grown to have a special love for the Jewish people. On a visit to Israel, I told a female Jewish soldier that America loves the Jewish people, and she replied, "The Jewish people love America."

I could speak those words because of my love and admiration for my good Jewish friend and Christian brother, Abe.

TESTING

God was doing so many wonderful things in our lives it was hard to digest everything. I recognized immediately some of the things He did, and some were incidents I didn't know, at least at the time, were orchestrated by God.

One such example was when I hired a new district manager, Mark Morton. He was single, but within two years of coming to work for me, he married a beautiful young lady from Costa Rica, Lucy Solano. Lucy is an international business development manager. After getting to know her, Jenny and I asked her to make some investments for us. We didn't know at the time, but God, in His providence, was allowing us to make investments that later in our lives would bless us and our finances tremendously.

God is a wonderful God and knows everything about our lives: past, present, and future. Jenny and I have learned to trust Him in every aspect of our lives. God sometimes places people into tight situations. We didn't know at the time, but

Jenny and I were going to go through one of those testing periods.

During those times, we all find out a lot about who we are and whether our commitments to trust God is a reality or merely words.

9

Life Lessons: Pieces of Transformation

What does it take for something to transform? For a seed to become a plant, it takes light. For a caterpillar to become a butterfly, it needs a cocoon. For a home to be renovated, it needs painting. The list can go on, but what do these have in common that answer the original question? *Time.* For Mike, the process of time created both beauty and brokenness. As you consider the lessons for this chapter, find the common theme that exists between all the pieces of the transformational puzzle of Mike's life.

Little Red Wagon

A wagon can carry the weight of the world, but
only the heart can carry the worth of a person.

Have you ever heard the phrase, "Mind your own little red wagon"? It is an old country way of saying mind your own business. Let me ask you: whose business do you mind? Mike describes a wrongly put together wagon that correctly showed his son as a top priority. What did Mike and his son use the wagon to do? Do you have a memory of your parents spending special times with you? If you are a parent, do you make the attempt to teach your children your values? Psalm 127:3–5 provides a picture of another type of "red wagon." What is it? What does this scripture say to you about your responsibility to mind your family business?

Time Table

A calendar may help capture our days,
but it is our Creator who should capture our moments.

Take a moment to read Philemon 1:6–7 and 1 Peter 3:15–16. What is the main subject of these verses? In this section, Mike described an opportunity to share the love of Christ. How did he do this? Have you ever had an opportunity like this, and if so, what did you do? When you share your faith in Christ, not everyone will readily accept what you say. What are you willing to do when this happens? Remember, it may take a long time for a decision for Christ to be made.

Bigger and Better

It is not the wide branches but the deep roots that
makes a tree able to withstand the winds of adversity.

At one of the company training meetings, Mike met a district manager named Abe. What was interesting about their initial conversation? What was Mike's response? Have you ever experienced someone making a stereotypical judgment on you? Have you done the same to others? Mike stated, "God is always working to fulfill his overall plans, and they are usually bigger and better than any of us could imagine." Do you agree with this statement? Why or why not? Why is it important to wait on God for the right timing to tell your salvation story? What are your thoughts on 2 Timothy 1:7–8?

Party of One

Taking a stand can make you feel strong.
It also can make you feel all alone.

Have you ever taken a stand for something right, only to feel as though you were alone in the crowd? Take a moment and reflect on the situation. Now answer this question: were you truly alone? Read Isaiah 43:1–5, and write down what the prophet teaches us about the presence of God. Are you willing to hold on to your convictions, even when pressured by those you regard as friends? How can you help others stand strong instead of going with the crowd?

Game of Twenty-One

The final tally of a man's score in the game of life is not found at the end of life but in the daily wins during life.

What are some responsibilities that keep you busy during the day? List them. Look over the list and ask yourself these questions: (1) what are the tasks that I must accomplish? (2) what are the tasks that I want to accomplish? (3) what are the tasks that I should be accomplishing?

Do you have your family on the list? Where did they fall? Mike made a decision to give his son a top place on his "list." Are you willing to do the same for your family, your core friends, and those God has called you to serve? Luke 10:38–42 provides for us a great reminder of the choices we make. What choice did each sister make? What choice will make a difference in your family life and your faith life?

The Picture

A messy life can simply be a masterpiece in the making.

Take a moment to read Ephesians 2:8–10. You may be familiar with the first two verses, but what about the last? What does it mean to be God's workmanship? Mike received his choice of his father's paintings. Which one did Mike choose? Why? If you could paint a picture to represent your life, what would it look like? Why?

Sense of Relief

Waiting to be forgiven or to forgive is like holding your breath.
It can make you blue in the end.

Throughout this book, you've read the damaging actions made by Mike's dad. What were some of them? Mike forgave his dad. Would you have been able to do the same? Why or why not? Who was touched by this decision? You may have experienced something similar in which you had to be the one willing to forgive. Read Acts 3:19 and Hebrews 10:17. What does God promise? What does it mean to you that there are no big I's and little yous at the foot of the cross? How can that affect how you view your faith life or someone else's?

Regional Manager

The position that you have is never as important
as the person you become while having it.

The growing responsibilities of Mike's job had costs. What were some of them? When you look back at your life and the choices you have made, what are some of the costs and blessings associated with your life choices? What did Mike promise Jenny he would do when they got married? Mike wanted to be baptized again when he and Jenny first attended First Baptist Church in Plant City, Florida. Why? How did Pastor Ron respond? Read Matthew 3:13–17 and Romans 6:3–6. What does baptism represent?

Precious Cargo

The life filled with precious memories and
moments usually has someone attached to it.

Have you ever seen a car with a sticker on the back that reads, "Precious cargo inside"? What does that mean? What value do you place on yourself? What about others? Mike went to be baptized earlier, but it did not happen. What happened because of the date change? In the time of rededicating his life, Mike's first act of service was to help a young child be baptized. Matthew 18:2–6 provides both promises and warnings. What are they?

Greatest Day

What we do for ourselves on this earth will fade
fast. Only those things done for God will last.

Mike shared a failing in his life—that he had not raised his son in church. What did Mike start praying for? Have you prayed for someone for the same reason? What has happened since you began praying for that person? In Joel 2:25–27, God promises restoration. What opportunity did God provide for Mike?

Mike called Steve's salvation one of the greatest moments of Mike's life. Have you experienced something similar? Reflect on how God provided an opportunity to share a restoration.

Courage

> It takes courage to allow someone to take the
> horizons you have created and expand them.

In your opinion, what does it mean to have your horizons expanded? When has this happened to you? Mike told about his friend Abe's salvation experience. Take a moment to read Acts 1:8. Mike stated, "God uses people, places, and time to accomplish His overall will." What ways has God used people, places, and time in your life?

Eulogy

> The only things a family takes away from a funeral
> are the words people said about the person.

Have you ever spoken at a funeral? What was the reason? Earlier, Mike made a promise to Abe to speak at his funeral.

Although Mike was unable to speak, why do you think it was important for him to write about this experience in this book? Read Luke 8:17 and 12:2. What does the Bible say about what is hidden?

Testing

*One does not have to fear a test when one has
studied well under a trusted teacher.*

Why does God test us? Can we be tested during the good times? Why or why not? In Psalm 30:7–9, we read a request from the author. What was it? Why would this request be an important step in trusting God in our tests? If the purpose of a test is to grow in knowledge, how have you grown in the knowledge of God through the different tests in your life?

CHAPTER 10

Pieces of Wealth and Wisdom

FAITH AND FINANCES

The year was 1997, and Steve, my son, was attending college at UCF in Orlando. Jenny and I had been married only a short time when she suggested we needed to start paying our tithe to the church. What she meant was, I needed to start paying my tithe. Jenny had been a tither all her adult life. My reply to her request was, "Do you know how much money it costs to keep Steve in school, not to mention the car, insurance, food, and housing? I can't afford to tithe, not now."

Jenny didn't debate the issue with me; she simply stated, "Isn't it amazing that we can trust God with our souls, but we can't trust Him with our finances?"

She left the room, and I sat in silence. I knew Jenny was correct. When you haven't been accustomed to paying a tithe, which is 10 percent of your income, it's hard to imagine how to work tithing into your budget. I reasoned that maybe after Steve graduated, I would start tithing. I sat in my office thinking about the many excuses why this was not possible, at least not right now. I was losing every argument I conceived. Jenny planted the seed, and it was weighing heavily on my heart.

THREE THINGS

The next Sunday, our teacher, Dub, asked to speak with me after class. I admired him greatly as a teacher and man of God. He asked if I would consider taking over teaching his class full time. He wanted to start working with young adults.

"I have never taught, except occasionally taking someone's place," I said.

"I've been praying about a replacement," Dub said. "My wife has prayed also. I asked her if God had placed a name upon her heart, and if so, who? She replied, 'Mike Simmons.' Mike, He placed your name on my heart too, before I talked to my wife."

I was almost speechless. Dub suggested I pray about his request and get back with him. I agreed, even though I thought I could never take Dub's class; I wasn't qualified.

When I told Jenny about the conversation, she asked, "What are you going to do?"

"I don't know," I replied.

During the next week, I spent much time in prayer, asking God to help me make the right decision. I needed His guidance. I felt completely inadequate and afraid to take on such a huge responsibility. I prayed, hoping God would excuse me from this responsibility, but instead He placed three thoughts on my heart.

1. He told me to commit to tithing, the very thing about which Jenny had spoken with me just a few weeks earlier.
2. He said for me to commit myself to serving Him. Dub had offered me an opportunity to serve, and it was clear I should set aside my fears, trust God, and take the class.
3. He said to become debt-free. That caught me off guard.

You may wonder if I only *thought* God spoke those words to my heart. Believe me; it would have been much easier if I could have said no to Dub and dismissed the whole idea about teaching. I couldn't do that. When God places something upon your heart, you can't ignore it, not if you ever want to have a peaceful night's sleep. I kept reviewing the three things over and over in my mind. I knew that one of these things couldn't be done on my own, and that was to become debt-free. That thought had never entered my mind until God placed it there. I wanted to please God, and I admit I was curious to see how God would work everything out, so this is what I did:

1. I went to my office, took out my checkbook, and laid it on my desk. I placed my hand over it and said, "Lord, I make this covenant with You to tithe our income until we have no money left." I followed that statement with, "However, based upon Your Word concerning tithing, that will never happen. You promised in Your Word to open the windows of heaven and pour out blessings that we cannot contain if we honor You with

our money. I believe Your promise is true. It belongs to me and to everyone who will follow up and accept Your invitation." I accepted God's invitation that day, and it truly was the smartest decision I have ever made.

2. I told the Lord, "I commit my service to You by teaching this class. I am afraid of being inadequate, but I rely upon Your Word: 'I can do all things through Christ who strengthens me.'" Subsequently I taught the class for eighteen years. I gave up the class in 2016 to work on this book, which I consider a tribute to God's faithfulness in Jenny's and my lives. He has taught Jenny and me many things about loving people, serving others, and trusting Him. Our lives have truly been enriched because of our commitments of service to God.

3. This is the one about becoming debt-free and solidified God's instructions to me. I said, "Lord, with Your help, I will do the first two things on Your list, but this third one will be up to You. I'm agreeing with You and trusting You to work out the details." About six weeks later, there was a knock on our door, and a man asked if we owned the property located to the east side of our house. When I said that we did, he asked, "Have you considered selling? I represent Lowe's, and we plan on building a new store on Highway 39. We would like to discuss purchasing your property."

Four months later we sold the house and property to Lowe's. We bought a new place to live, paid off everything, and became debt-free within a year of agreeing with God's instructions.

When I think about what God did, I feel overwhelmed with gratitude and am thankful for the opportunity to write about these events. I tell you these things not to brag but to share, with humility, these very personal events in our lives because I want you to see and believe in this great God we serve. I want you to know, as I do, that God is interested in you and is aware of everything happening in and around your life. He wants to and will be a part of your life, if you invite Him. Therefore, when God speaks to my heart, I move quickly. The world may listen to E. F. Hutton, but as for me and my family, we listen to God.

LOVING SACRIFICE

My mother in Arkansas became very ill and was diagnosed with cancer. Jenny and I drove home to spend a few days with the family. Mom loved Jenny, and Jenny loved Mother and treated her with great respect. It always meant a lot to me that my wife was respectful and kind toward my mom.

I will never forget all that Mother endured to keep us kids together. She worked hard and sacrificed a lot to make sure our lives were full. I am not saying that I loved Mother more or respected her more than my younger brother and sisters, but Tony and I, having gone through some very tough times with Mom, understood why she instilled in her children a belief that we could accomplish anything we set our minds to do. The words "I can't" were unacceptable to Mother.

I would sit by Mom's bed and talk with her for hours. She

was fascinated with talking about our favorite subject, heaven. Her heart was tender toward God, and I enjoyed sharing with her as much as she loved listening.

Byron and Tammy decided to move into Mother's house to take care of her. That was a major decision because the next five years of their lives were spent fulfilling that commitment. I told Byron that our family owed him and Tammy a great debt of gratitude, a debt we would never be able to repay. Mother did not want to live in a nursing home; if not for my brother and his wife, that is where she would have spent the last few years of her life. Byron and Tammy set an example for Jenny and me to follow, the extent of which we didn't realize at the time.

GLIMPSE OF HEAVEN

The day Mother passed away, we were all present, except for Tony. He was on his way home but didn't arrive in time. On the day of Mom's death, she had not spoken and her eyes remained closed. About one hour before she passed away, we were all gathered around her, singing some of her favorite Christian hymns, when suddenly she opened her eyes and spoke my name several times. It was as though she saw something that the rest of us could not see.

I remembered all the talks Mom and I shared about heaven, and perhaps she just wanted to tell me that it was all true. Maybe she got a glimpse of that beautiful place where she was going, or maybe she saw her heavenly escort. You may think I'm just exercising my imagination, and maybe I am, but it gives me great comfort, and it is my imagination. God is the one who said, through Paul, "But as it is written, Eye hath not seen, nor ear heard, neither have entered into the heart of man, the things which God hath prepared for them that love him" (1 Corinthians 2:9 KJV). My mother loved the Lord, and all things are possible with God.

I look forward to Mother's sharing with me someday what she was trying to say. I know Mother's reward in heaven is great. The sacrifices she made for her children throughout her life are almost unimaginable.

When this life is over, and if you have trusted in the Lord, there will never be separation of loved ones again. I am grateful for that. As the old hymn asks, will the circle be unbroken? That's a question only you can answer.

PRAYERS FOR PROVISIONS

There was a church in Plant City called Four Corners. I have always admired this church because they feed, clothe, and assist many homeless people in finding employment. One day while driving by the church, God spoke to my heart and told me to write them a check for a certain amount of money. I did not decide on the amount; God made it very clear to me.

I drove straight home, wrote a check for the amount I was told, and headed back to the church. When I knocked on the office door, there was no answer. I walked around outside to the kitchen and knocked on the screen door. A lady wearing a hairnet asked if she could help me.

"Ma'am, is the pastor here?" I asked.

"No, he's not."

"I have a check I want to give you," I said and handed it to her.

She yelled and called the names of other people, and soon there were four or five ladies present. She showed them the check, and they began jumping up and down. I couldn't help but start laughing. You would have thought I had handed them a check for a million dollars, but I assure you, I did not.

One of them said, "Oh sir, you don't realize why we are acting this way, so let me explain. This morning we knew many people would be coming for dinner today, but we did not have the money to buy food for all of them. We gathered in the middle of the kitchen, held hands, and prayed. We asked God for a miracle. We prayed that someone would be sent to supply our need—and here you are."

No matter how many times you see God work miracles, either for you or for someone through you, you never get accustomed to it. I walked back to my car after receiving hugs from those ladies. As I wiped the tears, I simply said, "God, you are magnificent. Thank you for letting Your children play a small part in Your overall plan." All my life I have heard it is more blessed to give than to receive. I have been on both ends of that spectrum, and they both give me cause to praise God.

Jenny and I had purchased a condominium and were doing some remodeling before we moved in. I mentioned to her that we needed to buy a new washer and dryer for the condo. Jenny is a very practical person and replied, "What's wrong with what we have? They work just fine."

I laughed and said, "Yes, but one is white and one is tan, and I want to get a matching set."

Jenny, being more practical in her thinking asked, "What will we do with the ones we have?"

A couple of weeks later, I decided to make another contribution to Four Corners Church. I knocked on the pastor's door and handed him a check.

As he sat back in his chair, he asked, "How would you like me to use this money?"

Not knowing the churches needs I replied, "Use it for whatever the need is."

"Maybe we can get a new washing machine," he said. "Ours is broken."

I could still hear Jenny's words ringing loudly in my ears, when she asked what will we do with the washer and dryer we have?

Trying not to show my astonishment to the pastors need, I asked, "If you need a washer, how about a dryer?"

"We need both."

I blurted out, "Does it matter if they match in color?"

"No, not if they work."

"Do you have access to a truck?" I asked. When he said that he did, I gave him my address and said, "Come by this afternoon, and I will give you a washer and a dryer."

God is such a wonderful God! He supplies our needs, and sometimes He supplies our wants. If we enjoy giving good gifts to our children, why do we not understand that God loves giving good gifts to His children also? That would be me, you, and, in this case, Four Corners Church.

Heart Pain

My friend Don Williamson—my boss when I first started working for the national baking company—called me to say he had decided to retire. I was happy for Don, but I knew that I would miss him greatly. I was regional manager of the southern end of Florida and Don had the northern end. We would share rides to all of our out-of-state meetings. He was a truly trusted friend. One of the things that concerned me and bothered me greatly about his retiring was that he had never given his heart to the Lord. I had known him for over twenty years but feared that I would not have the opportunity to spend much time with him after his retirement. Although we were friends, talking about trusting Jesus for salvation was not a topic he wanted to discuss. He was a nice guy and always said grace before our meals, but just being a good person doesn't get you to heaven.

Not long after Don retired, I was walking around the lake one day and felt a tightening in my throat. This had happened on several occasions. Jenny wanted me to mention it to our family doctor, but I didn't want to bother him.

Jenny, in her wisdom, thought it was important and decided to tell our doctor about the incident, so I went in for several tests. They told me I had blockage to my heart and needed to have open-heart surgery. I was shocked, but four days later I was wheeled into surgery and had a quadruple bypass. It was like nothing I had ever experienced in my life. I went from working out at the gym and pressing 250 pounds on a bench to not being able to shower on my own. I was off from work for five weeks and probably should have been off for at least seven weeks.

About a year after my surgery, my direct supervisor and I started having some differences. Our disagreements pertained to the treatment of some of my older district managers, things that I felt were not in compliance with the Equal Employment Opportunity Commission (EEOC) regulations. I refused to follow up with my supervisor's instructions and lost my job. They used a different reason for letting me go, but it was clear what had happened. I had worked for this company for almost twenty-five years. During that time, I never had a problem and always had very good evaluations.

I suddenly found myself unemployed for the first time in thirty-three years. I was separated from a company that I loved and greatly respected—and still do to this day. I was sixty-one years old and dazed, but I felt justified that I had made the correct decision by not breaking the EEOC rules. Sometimes you must do what you feel is appropriate, even if it costs you personally.

I didn't know what to do. I prayed about my circumstances because I couldn't quite figure out why this had happened as it did. I needed God to help me deal with the hurt, but I also needed His guidance. Jenny asked me to consult with an attorney named Joseph Dickerson, someone I knew locally. I drove to his office, and he agreed to see me without an appointment. When I described what had happened, he encouraged me to file a law suit, and he also arranged an appointment for me with an employment attorney in Tampa. He told me to pick him up the next morning, and he would attend the meeting with me. He was a friend and walked me through this traumatic event. I am very grateful for his counsel.

About five months later, we settled a federal lawsuit out-of-court, to our mutual satisfaction.

Right after I lost my job, I prayed and asked God to remember the covenant I made with Him concerning tithing our income. I said, "Lord, please don't let us tithe less than we did when I was working." God answered my prayer, and we always have been able to tithe above the amount we gave when I was employed.

GOING HOME

While all of this was going on, a friend, Evelyn Avery, became very ill. After a hospital stay, she was placed in a local nursing home. When we would visit, we often found her sitting in a wheelchair that had been placed in the lobby, with one sock on and one sock missing. She would be left there for several hours, and it was very uncomfortable for her. Her appetite diminished while at the home, and her weight dropped to around seventy-five pounds. Evelyn was close to ninety years old, and I knew she would not live long under those conditions.

One day when I visited Evelyn in the nursing home, she asked, "Mike, did you come to take me home?"

I shook my head. "Evelyn, I can't take you home. I don't have that authority."

She said, "I had a dream last night, and God told me you were going to take me home."

Jenny and I discussed the situation, and we agreed that

Evelyn needed help. We understood that for us to assume this responsibility meant moving into her house until she could make it on her own. That could be a long time, maybe never. I thought about my brother Byron and the sacrifice he and Tammy made for Mother. I admired them for what they did, never thinking Jenny and I would be faced with a similar situation. It was clear God had arranged our lives, from the loss of my job to where taking Evelyn home was a possibility. My mind kept going back to scripture: "And we know that all things work together for good to them that love God, to them who are called according to His purpose" (Romans 8:28).

The big question was whether we were willing to give up our time and freedom to make this commitment to our friend Evelyn. The facts were clear: she had no family, and there was no one to look after her. Should we leave her in a nursing home, or should we commit ourselves to taking care of her? After much discussion, Jenny and I committed to God and to one another to care for Evelyn, at no cost to her. Jenny had known Evelyn and her late husband, Keith, for fifty years. Jenny had a special love for Evelyn, and although I didn't know at the time, I would grow to love her too.

Evelyn was thrilled to be back in her house. She had a beautiful view of the lake and the ducks and birds. I would open the blinds, and she would sit for hours and watch people walk up and down the walking path outside of her window. Jenny and I had our routine. I would fix breakfast for Evelyn, read the paper to her, and fix lunch. Jenny would relieve me around 1:00 p.m., and I had the afternoon to go home and do whatever I needed to do around our house. We stayed with Evelyn twenty-four hours a day for the first six months.

When she got better, we would go home at night and then come back the next morning to awaken her. This went on for several years.

WORLD BY THE TAIL

My friend Don would call me from time to time just to talk about old times. During one particular call, he mentioned how much he loved retirement. He said, "Mike, I have the world by the tail and not a care in the world." He talked of some investments he had made with his 401(k) account, money that afforded him the opportunity to do pretty much anything he wanted to do from a financial perspective. He told me he had bought a new pickup truck and had paid cash—forty-eight thousand dollars—for it. He said his life was great. I told him how happy I was for him.

No more than six weeks later, Don's son called to inform me that Don had suffered an aneurysm and was paralyzed on his left side. His speech was slurred, but you could make out what he was saying if you listened carefully.

I called Don and asked if I could visit him. He was living in a nursing home in Orange Park, Florida. He asked me not to come. I could tell he was very depressed. He said, "I don't want anyone to see me in this condition." I tried to persuade him to let me visit but realized I should wait until he got better.

UNTO THESE

I loved to walk around Walden Lake—twice around the lake equaled approximately four miles, and I could walk it in about an hour. We had been caring for Evelyn for about nineteen months. Her condition had become much worse, to the point that she needed full-time attention for all her needs. I would get her up, change her, tend to her personal needs, cook her breakfast, wash the dishes, read the paper to her, and then get her settled for a nap.

On this day I decided to go for the four-mile walk around the lake. I like to use the walk for my prayer time. I said, "Lord, I can't quite understand my life. Just a few months ago I held the job of regional manager for a major corporation, with many people reporting to me, a job that I held for over twenty-four years. Now I tend to the daily needs of a ninety-two-year-old woman. Lord, I don't understand."

God spoke plainly to my heart. He said, *"The job you held as regional manager was a job that was important to the world, but what you are doing for Evelyn is important to me."* I settled in my mind that day that I was where God wanted me to be.

Our time on this earth is very short compared to eternity, and what we do in Jesus's name is all that really counts.

THE EXTENSION

On Thursday of that week I received a call from Don's son. He told me his dad had been diagnosed with a malignant brain tumor, and the doctors did not expect him to live past the weekend. I started walking and praying. I said, "Lord, I know Don is not saved, and I also know, it is not Your will that any should perish. If You will spare his life and give him a little more time, I will go to Orange Park on Monday and offer Don the plan of salvation."

I told Jenny what had happened with Don, and she agreed that I should go. God, in His mercy, spared Don's life through the weekend, and on Monday morning I headed to the nursing home where he was staying. Don and I talked for a long time. He told me he knew his life was over and he had only a short time to live. He said, "I thought I had everything I needed, and now I have nothing; it's all gone."

I talked with Don about the plan of salvation, and for the first time, he listened. I told him that he could accept Jesus as his Savior, and God would save him and give him a home in heaven. I said, "Don, would you like to pray a sinner's prayer with me? It's a prayer that all Christians, including me, have prayed. It's a simple prayer of faith, asking God to forgive you of your sins."

Don reached out his hand to me. Through his tears, he said, "I'm ready, buddy."

We prayed together, and Don placed his faith and trust in Christ for the forgiveness of his sins. I thank God for His mercy in sparing Don for a few extra days and giving him another opportunity. About a week later, I received the call; Don had passed-away. God truly is merciful and not willing that any should perish. I think about Don often. I look forward to seeing him again someday. We will be able to talk, laugh, and share with one another all the joys of living and serving our glorious God.

ETERNAL ASSUMPTIONS

Jenny and I continued in our commitment to care for Evelyn and make her life as full as possible. We drove her around town at Christmastime so she could see all the holiday decorations. We often drove by many of her friends' homes, and no matter how they were decorated, she declared them beautiful. We usually ended our evenings by getting a milkshake. Evelyn would only take a few sips and then say, "Don't throw it away; I'll finish it tomorrow."

I was still teaching Sunday school while attending to Evelyn. She would often ask me to read my lessons to her. She loved for me to read and would listen attentively. In addition to the morning paper, I also read different books of the Bible to her, and I would sometimes review my Sunday school lesson at her request. She had a sharp mind and understood exactly whatever I read.

One day we were talking about salvation. During the conversation, she stated several times, "I hope I go to heaven." After making that statement on more than one occasion, I said, "Eve, why do you say you hope to go to heaven? Don't you know you are going to heaven?"

She looked at me with tears in her eyes and said, "I hope I go, but I've never done anything worthy enough to get me there." It was at that moment I realized that Evelyn had attended church her entire life but didn't completely understand salvation and its requirements. Everyone just assumed that at her age she understood.

I moved my chair over by her rocker and said, "Eve, there is no one here but you, me, and God. Will you pray a prayer with me so you can know that you are going to heaven, and you will never doubt your salvation again?" I offered her my hands, and she coupled them with hers. She prayed with me that morning, and I then fully understood why God had placed Jenny and me with Evelyn. God was correct; this job of getting to know and love Evelyn was much more important than any job we had ever held.

We called hospice because Evelyn had lost weight and was back down to around seventy-five pounds. She took all her meals in bed, and we knew her remaining time with us was short. I would sit in her bedroom and read to her. Our senior pastor, Brian Stowe, and our senior adult pastor, Claud Walker, came by to visit with Evelyn near the end. She enjoyed their visit so much. She referred to Pastor Brian as "that handsome little boy." I guess when you're ninety-three you can refer to people any way you wish. Evelyn meant it as a great compliment; Pastor Brian likely will cherish her proclamation of his youth in about fifteen more years. I realized, through Evelyn's enthusiasm, that visiting our senior adults means so much to them. Just for them to know that we care enriches their lives and brightens their days.

Evelyn had no children and no immediate family. Jenny, however, loved her with the love of a daughter. I am thankful that we could keep Evelyn in her home during her final years. We became her family and treated her with love and respect. In the end, we blessed her, and she blessed us in ways that we never expected.

10

Life Lessons: Pieces of Wealth and Wisdom

What does true wealth look like to you? In this chapter, Mike put the final pieces of the Blue House puzzle into place. It not only revealed the picture of his life story, but it also might help to uncover some of the same experiences you may have in yours. As you consider these questions, remember that the beginning of wisdom starts with the awe of the Lord.

Faith and Finances

A man with his money is like a child with his toy;
both possess a death grip that will never turn loose.

Mike's wife, Jenny, told Mike, "Isn't it amazing we can trust God with our souls, but we can't trust Him with our finances?" In the area of finances and tithing, how would you rate your trust level with God? Is it full trust, some trust, or little trust? God gives us a multitude of blessings in life, yet we often have a hard time blessing Him back. Read Malachi 3:6–12, and write down God's position on tithing.

Three Things

It is not the number of steps you need to right a wrong
in life that is important. It is simply the willingness
to take the first step to get it started.

Have you ever been asked to serve God in a special way? Did you prepare with delight, or did you wish the world would end before you had to do it? Mike was asked by his friend, Dub, to teach a Bible study class. What was Mike's reaction? What did Mike do in response to the three things God told him to do? How do you measure up with these steps? Deuteronomy 28:12–13 gives a biblical view on debt. What are we expected to do and not do regarding our finances? How can you demonstrate that decision this week?

Loving Sacrifice

When you are willing to put your life on hold, you help others so they don't have to put their lives on hold.

In this section, Mike's mom became too weak to live by herself. Her son Byron and his wife volunteered to move in with her. What did the move cost them? What example did they demonstrate for the family? Would you be willing to make that sacrifice? Read Mark 10:28–30. What does this passage mean to you regarding your willingness to sacrifice for God?

Glimpse of Heaven

Heaven is seen with the heart before it is seen with the eyes.

Read Revelation 22:1–5. As Mike and his family were with his mom before she passed away, she suddenly opened her eyes and spoke Mike's name several times. Have you experienced a time when someone's face reflected the glory of God's presence as he or she passed away? Mike expressed a thought found in 1 Corinthians 2:7–9. What was it? How have you prepared for heaven?

Prayers for Provision

Before we reach out for help in programs, we
need to reach up for help in prayer.

Have you ever asked God for something and then, in a matter of minutes, He answered? How did you react? God impressed upon Mike that he should give to a local mission church. How did it impact the workers at the church? Has God ever used you to bless someone's life when he or she prayed for help? Philippians 4:6–7 encourages all Christians to pray. Why? For what have you asked God? How has He answered your prayers?

Heart Pain

The heart can hurt for two reasons: one is a lack of blood
and oxygen; the other is a lack of belief and morals.

Mike suffered a variety of setbacks during this time in his life. With which one can you identify, and why? Mike lost physical ability due to a heart condition. He lost his job because of a moral decision. Would you have been willing to do the right thing, even if it cost you your job? As you read Romans 5:3–5, consider your character. What do people see in you? Character is one of the most important things you have. How are you developing yours?

Going Home

Home is more than where you hang
your heart; it is your heart.

Have you ever completed a trip and were glad to be back home? I've been in the hospital due to a surgery and felt I would heal better once I came home. Home is a powerful place for comfort and security, healing and hope. Mike shared that he and Jenny decided to bring Evelyn back to her home from the nursing home. How did coming home help her? What was the big question that Mike and Jenny had to answer? Read Proverbs 3:27 and Luke 6:38. How do these verses relate to the decision Mike and Jenny made?

World by the Tail

That of which we think we have control will,
in the end, control us.

Have you ever met someone who seemed to have everything he or she needed or wanted? How did that person make you feel? Don told Mike that he had everything he needed or wanted. In 1 Timothy 6:17–19, what did Paul say about riches? What happens if your significance is wrapped up in what you have, rather than in who you are?

Unto These

When you give to those in need, you deposit riches into the account of God that will provide eternal dividends for you.

While walking around the lake, Mike reflected on his life. What job was important to him? What job was important to God? When you see where you are in life, can you trace the hand of God that brought you there? In Hebrews 6:9–12, what is the importance of serving where God wants? What decision are you perhaps struggling with right now regarding doing things your way or God's way?

The Extension

The chance to get our houses in order is not only a gift of time;
it is a gift of grace.

Second Kings 20:1–8 provides a story of King Hezekiah and the extension of his life. In this section, Mike asked God to extend the life of his friend Don. Why? What happened as a result of that prayer? Have you ever asked God to do something special like that? In James 4:13–17, our lives are called a mist or a vapor. What should we do in the time we have? Are you willing to do it?

Eternal Assumptions

Eternity is a long time to get something wrong.

Have you ever been surprised by people coming to know the Lord in their older years? A person may have been a member of the church for most of his or her life. Mike was given an opportunity to talk with Evelyn about her salvation. What was it that prompted him to ask? How can a person know for sure he or she is saved? Romans 10:13 assures us that all who call on the name of the Lord will be saved. How would you share with them the good news of God's grace?

CHAPTER 11

Final Pieces

PIECES OF THE PRESENT

The year was 2011, and Jenny and I had gone back to Hoxie and Walnut Ridge, Arkansas, for vacation. We always stayed with my brother Byron and his wife, Tammy. They usually closed their business, Bloominfield's Lawn and Garden, just to spend time with us. We have always appreciated their hospitality in making us feel welcome. Byron and I were discussing some of the changes to their city when he broke the shattering news to me. The famous Blue House had been torn down.

As you know by now, the Blue House was a very special place in my life. As a kid, when things in my life were almost too difficult to bear, I would retreat to my memories of the Blue House. Those memories gave me a sense of safety, a sense of belonging and security. It was just a little blue house, now almost sixty years ago, but to me it represented the happiest time of my childhood, and I hated to think about its being torn down.

I purposely waited a few days before driving by what was now an empty lot. I had visited the Blue House on every trip home for the past forty years. I thought about buying the house and restoring it to its glory days of 1957, but reality set in after discussing this project with Jenny.

PIECES OF THE PAST

When I drove down the street where the Blue House had been located, we passed the home economics building where, as a six-year-old, I threw a rock at Tony and busted a pane in the French door of the entrance. We turned right at Dolly Smith's Corner Store, where in years past I bought those famous lemon cookies. There, in my sights, was the yellow-block school building and playground, where I spent hours of my young life chasing out-of-bounds balls for the older boys. I slowed down the car as we approached the empty lot where the Blue House had stood. It had been built on that lot before I was born, and now it was gone and would never come back. It had been an earthly treasure to me.

Now, sitting in the car, looking at the empty lot, my mind went to the words Jesus spoke in Matthew[6:19–21.KJV] "Do not lay up for yourselves treasures on earth where moth and rust destroy and where thieves brake in and steal; but lay up for yourselves treasures in heaven. For where your treasure is there your heart will be also."

PIECES OF THE FUTURE

As I looked at the empty lot where the Blue House had been, I remembered that the house had needed costly repairs in recent years. The roof was in bad shape, the sidewalk was cracked, and the paint was chipped so badly it was hard to tell it had been painted blue. It had served its purpose as temporary residence for temporary people.

I realized we are just like the old blue house. We are temporary, and this world is not our home. We are just passing through into eternity. At that moment, with great joy, I remembered John [14:2.KJV]

> In my Father's house are many mansions; if it were not so, I would have told you. I go to prepare a place for you. And if I go and prepare a place for you, I will come again and receive you to myself; that where I am, there you may be also.

The Blue House was just that—a blue house. It grew old and was torn down. In my heavenly Father's house, I have a place Jesus Himself has prepared for me. Because it was prepared just for me, I can allow my imagination to run wild, knowing it will be perfect.

AFTERWORD

I hope you have enjoyed reading real-life stories about my family and me. The pages of this book tell about my everyday life, and the memories were sometimes very difficult for me to consider and even more difficult to write. Perhaps you can see and appreciate, as I do, God's faithfulness to our family. He is a wonderful God, who desires to be involved in the assembling of the pieces of our life puzzles. For Christians, He is the central piece. Sadly, non-Christians live and die with that central piece to their life puzzles missing.

I want to finish the book with a true story about a man named Jack Harris, which was told by international author, teacher, and pastor David Jeremiah. When I read the story in the Turning Point daily devotional book *Hope for Today*, I felt that it completed all that I had been trying to portray throughout my book concerning God's presence in the final picture of our lives. Without Him, we are missing the one thing that makes life worth living. It's called [The Central Piece]. The British newspaper, the Sun, ran a story about Jack Harris, age eighty-six, who spent seven years working on a huge jigsaw puzzle of five thousand pieces, only to discover that the last piece was missing. He was devastated, especially when he learned that the puzzle was no longer in production so there was no chance of finding a replacement. The puzzle was a picture of French artist James Tissot's 1862 painting, *Return of the Prodigal Son.* Fortunately, the public outcry caused the *Sun* to commission a perfect copy of the final piece, and photographers were on hand when Jack snapped it into place.

How many of us are laboring away at life, day and night, growing old, trying to piece together the puzzle of life? How many get to the end, only to realize that they're missing the key piece of it all?

Christ is the central piece and the central peace of life. His pardon covers our faults. His promises ensure our future. His purpose gives meaning to life, and His providence guides our steps. Christ's providence reaches across the world, throughout all time and into each of our lives. In Him, I am complete. Are you?

If you have any questions or thoughts to share or have made a decision for Christ, I invite you to communicate with me through my private E-Mail address mds14841@gmail.com. I look forward to hearing from you.

FINAL APPLICATIONS

The Box Top Revisited

As we conclude the study of *The Blue House*, Mike provided the last three pieces of the puzzle—the past, the present, and the future. How do the memories of the Blue House resonate with your own experiences of home, family, and friends? In finishing a puzzle, it is the next puzzle piece that creates anticipation toward completion. Let us begin with the present.

Pieces of the Present

Every day is God's gift to us. That is
why it is called the "present."

What does it mean to be present when you are with others? In our daily lives, we will have multiple opportunities to experience the here and now. Take a moment to read Ecclesiastes 3:1–8. In the list given by the scripture, where are you today? Why?

Pieces of the Past

Those who only live in the past cannot thrive
in the future because they have no present.

The past can be a wonderful thing on which to reflect, to tell about, and to draw from, but to be stuck there creates problems for us. It is the difference between driving a car and looking in the rearview mirror to see where you have been or looking forward through the windshield to see where you are going. Mike provided reflections from his past. What are some of yours? How have they helped you in the present to prepare for the future? Do you have any memories that are still holding you back? Read Ecclesiastes 1:9–14 to see what truly helps us to live in the present and prepare for the future.

Pieces of the Future

We never have to worry about our lives going to pieces
when we trust the Creator with all of the pieces.

Throughout this book, Mike provided memories that serve as pieces of his life. What piece was the most important for him? What is yours? Mike chose his spiritual "pieces" as his priority. How do you feel mainstream society thinks about spiritual priorities? Revelation 7:9–17 tells about the future for Christians. Are you ready for the future? You are ready if Christ is the central piece and the central peace of your life.

ABOUT THE AUTHORS

Michael Simmons joined the US Army National Guard at the age of nineteen, where he proudly served his country for six years. He was employed for five years by General Electric Corporation, where he became an active member of the AFL-CIO union. Michael was appointed by Arkansas governor David Prior to serve as Deputy Director of Labor for the state of Arkansas. He was employed as a personnel analyst with the city of Saint Petersburg, Florida, where he worked in conjunction with the federal EEOC, monitoring the minority hiring practices of the Saint Petersburg Police and Fire Departments.

In 1979 Mike joined the ranks of the self-employed, running his own food distribution business for seven years. He was hired by a national food manufacturing company to serve as a district manager. He was soon promoted to a regional sales manager, positions he held for twenty-four years.

Michael enjoyed teaching an adult co-ed Sunday school class at the First Baptist Church in Plant City, Florida, for eighteen years. He is currently an active member of the

International Gideon Society. Michael also serves on the board of directors for HUD-sponsored senior housing: the Family Living Center and the Towers of Plant City, Florida.

 Dr. Daniel Middlebrooks has over thirty years of chaplaincy, pastoral, and military-level experience in leading and ministering to both civilian and multi-faith military organizations, ranging from three hundred to ten thousand. His military career culminated with his serving as the senior instructor and course manager/developer for the United States Chaplain Center and School, Chaplain Captain's Career Course at Fort Jackson, South Carolina.

He currently serves as the Command Chaplain for the Hillsborough County Sheriff's Office, Tampa Florida. He has also served as the senior pastor of Hopewell Baptist Church, Plant City, Florida and vice president of leadership development for the Biblical Leadership Institute, Plant City, Florida. He continues to serve as the chaplain for Plant City, Florida, the Hillsborough County School Board Security Division, and numerous other organizations in the Tampa/ Plant City area. He is the CEO/president of R3 Care & Consulting, LLC, and Chaplaincy Care, Inc. He has become a sought-after relationship leader in business, marriage, and life transitions. He is the author of *Strategic Methods for a Successful Marriage.*

Dr. Middlebrooks and his wife of twenty-nine years, Arienne, have two daughters, Erica and Allison, and reside in Plant City, Florida, in the home of his birth.

CPSIA information can be obtained
at www.ICGtesting.com
Printed in the USA
LVOW07*0331210617
538829LV00018B/575/P